CHARLES
RICHET

A Nobel Prize Winning Scientist's Exploration of Psychic Phenomena

CHARLES RICHET

A Nobel Prize Winning
Scientist's Exploration of
Psychic Phenomena

by

CARLOS S. ALVARADO, PhD

WHITE CROW

www.whitecrowbooks.com

Praise for
Charles Richet

In the history of Western psychology, William James, Wilhelm Wundt, and Charles Richet stand out as its acknowledged founders, but it was Richet who bridged academic psychology and its applications in psychotherapy. In this remarkable book, Carlos Alvarado discloses another of Richet's bridges, the link between his background in psychophysiology and his interest in psychical research. It was Richet who first applied statistical evaluation to the identification of hidden targets, and who proposed a sophisticated psychological explanation of mediumship. These and other contributions reveal a mind that was visionary yet disciplined; one whose insights are still relevant in the twenty-first century.

STANLEY KRIPPNER, PH.D., CO-EDITOR,
VARIETIES OF ANOMALOUS EXPERIENCE.

Dr. Carlos S. Alvarado is a consummate scholar, researcher and historian evident by his choice of Charles Richet essays. Like Richet, he is fearless in his subject matter and with years of scholarly reading brings insight and clear thinking within the complex study of psychical phenomena.

I heartily recommend *Charles Richet: A Nobel Prize Winning Scientist's Explorations of Psychic Phenomena.*

LISETTE COLY, PRESIDENT,
PARAPSYCHOLOGY FOUNDATION

Charles Richet belongs to that most select group of individuals, including Marie Curie and William James, whose genius flowed over disciplinary borders and whose insatiable interests included psi phenomena. Richet, Nobel prize winner in physiology, innovative experimentalist, writer whose play's title role Circé was performed by Sarah Bernhardt, and founder of parapsychology research in France, finds a splendid chronicler in Carlos S. Alvarado, our foremost contemporary historian of parapsychology.

ETZEL CARDEÑA, PH. D., THORSEN PROFESSOR
OF PSYCHOLOGY AT LUND UNIVERSITY,
SWEDEN, AND CO-EDITOR OF *PARAPSYCHOLOGY: A HANDBOOK FOR THE 21ST CENTURY AND VARIETIES OF ANOMALOUS EXPERIENCE.*

Carlos Alvarado is well qualified to write this book. Analyzing Charles Richet's contributions to psychical research is a difficult challenge because of epistemological biases that prevent us applying the usual scholarly approach. Alvarado has patiently collected every document relative to his topic and presented them in a clear didactic way, and in context. This book was deeply needed.

RENAUD EVRARD, PhD, UNIVERSITÉ DE LORRAINE, AUTHOR, *LA LÉGENDE DE L'ESPRIT: ENQUÊTE SUR 150 ANS DE PARAPSYCHOLOGIE* (2016).

Charles Richet was a leading representative of the French life sciences and early experimental psychology. As a historical figure, he is notoriously difficult to pigeonhole. A Nobel Laureate in physiology/medicine and aviation pioneer, Richet was a glowing pacifist while also advocating eugenics and a disturbing 'scientific racism'. A devout epiphenomenalist incapable of taking seriously the idea of discarnate minds, he was France's pre-eminent investigator of parapsychological phenomena. Richet still awaits a biographer doing justice to all of his multi-faceted and seemingly contradictory interests and activities. In the meantime, these essays by Carlos S. Alvarado will be an indispensable and convenient starting point for anybody interested in Richet's métapsychique.

ANDREAS SOMMER, PhD, AUTHOR OF *CROSSING THE BOUNDARIES OF MIND AND BODY: PSYCHICAL RESEARCH AND THE ORIGINS OF MODERN PSYCHOLOGY* (PHD THESIS, UNIVERSITY COLLEGE LONDON)

An interesting book on the Nobel Prize winning physiologist Charles Richet (1950-1935) and his contributions to psychical research. In his classic *Traité de Métapsychique* (1922), Richet gives an overview of this field, which he called métapsychique. He attempted to explain mental phenomena such as telepathy with his concept of cryptesthesia, involving brain functioning, and was critical of survival research. This book is a valuable contribution to the pre-WWII history of psychical research.

ERLENDUR HARALDSSON, PhD, PROFESSOR EMERITUS, UNIVERSITY OF ICELAND, AUTHOR OF *I SAW A LIGHT AND CAME HERE: CHILDREN'S EXPERIENCES OF REINCARNATION* (WITH J. MATLOCK), AND *INDRIDI INDRIDASON THE ICELANDIC PHYSICAL MEDIUM* (WITH L. GISSURARSON).

It is little known today that the French scientist Charles Richet, by analyzing a wide range of anomalous manifestations of the human psyche, performed influential studies that affected the development of psychical research. This book by Carlos Alvarado, the first one published in English about Richet's psychical research, is of utmost importance as it examines the work carried out by Richet and the results he achieved applying a rigorous and scientific approach to the phenomena. The volume provides much useful information about important aspects of the history of psychical research between nineteenth and twentieth century, and offers historical insights on a notable border area of the culture.

MASSIMO BIONDI, MD, AUTHOR OF *TAVOLI E MEDIUM: STORIA DELLO SPIRITISMO IN ITALIA*, AND *LA RICERCA PSICHICA*.

Contents

~

In memory of my parents, Ileana Vélez and
Carlos M. Alvarado, for their love, support, and
understanding.

Introduction

～

One of the issues of the proceedings of the *Académie des Sciences* for 1922 recorded the presentation of a book to that august body. The author hoped that the "irregular and singular facts" contained in the work would be considered worthy of study instead of being met with "sarcasm and silent disdain" (Richet, 1922a, p. 429; this, and other translations, are mine). The topics of the book were phenomena that "are new; they are inhabitual; they are difficult to classify" (p. 430). The author continued by stating: "The word metapsychics ... which I created to designate this science of occult things ... indicates that the phenomena are of a psychological order, but they exceed common classic psychology, and enlarge enormously the field of human intelligence" (pp. 429–430).

This was physiologist Charles Richet (1850–1935), presenting his *Traité de Métapsychique* (1922b), an overview of psychical research, a field that Richet referred to as metapsychics (on this aspect of Richet see the bibliographies in Appendix E.). By 1922 Richet, one of the most eminent of French scientists ever involved with the study of psychic phenomena, was already well known as a physiologist, as well as a student of various disciplines and topics. The essays presented here will focus on his psychical research.

Richet's eminence in various disciplines was established before 1922. In addition to various physiological and medical investigations, he was known for his Nobel Prize in 1913 for his work in anaphylaxis. (For overviews of Richet's life and work see van Wijland, 2015, and Wolf, 1993). But Richet was active in many other areas as well. He has been called one of the great thinkers of France (Painlevé, 1926) and discussed as a person who "was often at the forefront of modernity in various forms: he was an inventor, explorer, defender of justice, and a man of letters" (Carroy, 2004, p. 245). Richet wrote poetry and plays, many under the name of Ch. Epheyre. But he also wrote about general history, medical bibliography, philosophical issues, physiology, psychical research, psychology, social problems, world peace, and was involved in aviation (Carroy, 2004; Wolf, 1993).

Richet has been considered by many to be a Renaissance man. A colleague psychical researcher commented that Richet was a well-balanced man and an ideal European (Sudre, 1935). He was, in the view of fairly recent writers,

> Independent, open and tolerant, engaging with courage in science, in thought and in noble causes even though the positions exposed him to public opinion because he had courage. He remained always himself ... physician, researcher and humanist, his

successes and mistakes indicating his time (Richet
& Estingoy, 2003, p. 509).

By the time Richet started publishing about psychic
phenomena, there was a large body of literature about
mesmerism, Spiritualism, and psychic phenomena in
general, as seen in various overviews of these topics
(see Appendix F.). Among other institutions, the
Society for Psychical Research (SPR) was founded in
England in 1882, which produced many studies about
telepathy, apparitions, mediumship, and dissociative
phenomena of different sorts (Alvarado, 2002; Gauld,
1968). This period produced much empirical work about
psychic phenomena, of which Richet was a contributor.
Similarly, Richet was part of this movement, particularly
strong in France, that explored the existence and range
of non-conscious human functioning and that included
both conventional and unconventional phenomena
(Plas, 2000).

In this book I present general information about
Richet's psychical research work, a field that he called
metapsychics. My purpose is not to present a systematic
study of Richet's psychic interests, but to make more
accessible my previously published essays about Richet's
work in this area, which appeared in specialized
journals. I hope that what I discuss in the following
chapters will allow my readers to obtain a general
impression of the scope of Richet's work in this field
(particularly the general review appearing in the first
chapter), and to learn something about some of his
particular contributions. To assist in this endeavor I
have compiled, with Renaud Evrard, a bibliography of
writings about Richet's psychic work, and of Richet's
own writings (see Appendix E.).

Interest in Psychic Phenomena

~

Charles Robert Richet was one of the most eminent scientists of the past to be involved in psychical research. He was also a man who explored different areas of knowledge. It was once said of him that:

> In all France there is not at this moment so admirably typical a Frenchman as Professor Charles Richet … Professor Richet is a member of the Academy of Medicine, Professor of Medicine, Editor of the great Dictionary of Physiology, a *savant* of the first rank. He is more than a scientist. He is a man, a citizen of the world, cosmopolitan, international, and yet, in his essence, distinctively, delightfully French (Anonymous, 1905, p. 240).

More recently, he has been referred to as an individual who "was often at the forefront of modernity in various forms: he was an inventor, explorer, defender of justice, and a man of letters" (Carroy, 2004, p. 245).

A Brief Biography

Richet was born in 1850 in Paris, into a family of high social standing. His father, Alfred Richet, (1816-1891) taught surgery at the Faculté de Médicine in Paris, and was a member of the Académie des Sciences. His mother's family was also distinguished: Eugénie Renouard (1827-1884) was the daughter of Charles Renouard (1794-1878), an eminent lawyer and a Peer of France. Richet became a physician in 1869 and, in 1878, obtained a doctorate in science. At the Faculté de Médicine, he became an *agrégé* in 1878, and was Professor of Physiology from 1887 until his retirement. Later honors included memberships of the Académie de Médicine (1898) and the Académie des Sciences (1914), a Nobel Prize in 1913 for his work in anaphylaxis, and a Legion of Honor Award (1926). Richet married Amélie Aubry (1856-1953) in 1877 and died in 1935 in Paris (For biographical information see Wolf, 1993).

Richet was well-known as a physiologist. He was described in an 1879 medical journal as "One of the rising younger Frenchmen of scientific tastes and ability, already the author of several works of merit" (Putnam, 1879, p. 815).

In addition to the work that was the focus of his Nobel Prize, Richet worked on topics such as the chemical properties of gastric juice, excitability of muscles, serum therapy, and animal heat. (For a bibliography see Wolf, 1993). In addition, he was involved in aviation, wrote plays and poetry (some under the pseudonym Ch. Epheyre), and published papers and books on topics such as history, pacifism, philosophy, psychical research, sociology, and world peace (Carroy, 2004; Wolf, 1993). Examples of some of this other work are his writings *Soeur Marthe* (as Epheyre, 1889), *Les Guerres et la Paix* (1899), *Circé* (1903; with R. Brund), *Abregé d'Histoire Générale* (1919a), *La Selection Humaine* (1919b) and "L'Aviation Triomphante" (1926).

Richet saw psychology as an extension of physiology. In his *Essai de Psychologie Générale* (1887), he explored instinct, memory, ideas, and will. He argued that: "The basis of psychology is … the knowledge of the laws that rule the nervous system." Consequently, for Richet, the first task of psychology was the study of the "conditions of existence of the apparatus that produces intelligence" (Richet, 1887, p. 55).

Published in different journals, some of his early writings about such topics as disgust, drugs, pain, demonic possession, hypnosis, hysteria, and "man as the ruler of animals" were presented in *L'Homme et l'Intelligence* (1884a), conceptualized by him as "fragments of physiology and psychology." Richet was conscious of humans being different from animals—able to modify and eventually understand their environment. "King of living beings," he wrote, "man has managed to still be the king of natural forces. … He is the king of animals, but he is an animal king. This is not a human kingdom: this is the kingdom of man." (Richet, 1884a, p. 454).

Starting in 1875, he published discussions and research about hypnosis that stimulated later work on the subject (Richet, 1875). Some of the common phenomena he listed were hallucinations, and the loss of memory during the hypnotic state. In his view: "Comparing the somnambulistic state to certain physiological phenomena now well known, we can assume that there is inhibition of parts of the brain that govern the will and memory" (Richet, 1884a, p. 259).

Richet helped to popularize the view that the dramatic convulsions and hallucinations of the grand hystero-epileptic attack were similar to some of the old descriptions of the signs of demonic possession; also that hysterics suffered from a lack of will to control their emotions, and were open to contagion by imitation (Richet, 1880). Furthermore, he explored empirically what he referred to as the "objectification of types", or changes of personality during hypnosis, with amnesia of the usual personality resulting from suggestion. Such cases suggested to Richet that there was a "dissociation of the psychic elements" of personality (Richet, 1883, p. 233) in which memory and imagination were affected.

In addition to developing the physiological side of nineteenth-century psychology, Richet was active in other ways in psychology. Earlier in 1885 he had been one of the founding members, and later the General Secretary of the Société de Psychologie Physiologique that was presided over by Jean-Martin Charcot (1825–1893). In meetings of this society, Richet presented on such varied topics as somnambulism induced at a distance, and suggestion (Richet, 1886b, 1886d). Working within the Société, Richet was an important figure in the organization of the *Congrès International de Psychologie Physiologique* that met at Paris during the Universal Exposition in 1889. Richet was the General Secretary of the Congress and continued to participate in future meetings (on the congresses, and Richet's participation in them see Alvarado, 2017).

Being a pacifist, Richet wrote in his *Les Guerres et la Paix* that war "consumes the energies and forces of nature without profit" (Richet, 1899, p. 160).

Interestingly, he believed it was necessary to get rid of the undesirable in order to improve the human race, a topic that he discussed in his book *La Sélection Humaine* (1919b). Societal norms, he argued, interfered with natural selection, allowing the undesirable to survive. In his view, there should be a mechanism for the social selection of people based on their intelligence, health, beauty, and other positive characteristics. Richet was aware that this view would be shocking and unacceptable to many.

Initial Steps in Psychical Research

Richet wrote that his first observation of possible psychic functioning occurred in 1872 when he was a medical student (see Chapter 2). This was an instance of what later became known as ESP (a term Richet did not use). A hypnotized young woman named Mariette was asked about the name of another medical student at the school and she said: "There are five letters. The first is H, the second if E; I cannot see the third ... The fourth ... is R; and the fifth N" (Richet, n.d. b, p. 68). The name was Hearn.

In 1873 Richet also reported his successful attempts to send commands at a distance to a female patient while he was a medical intern. In his article, Richet concluded: "If, therefore, the phenomenon exists—and I think it is difficult to deny it absolutely—it is extremely rare, and occurs only in special circumstances which so far elude scientific determination" (Richet, 1886b, p. 200).[1]

His first articles on psychic phenomena were published in the 1880s. These included observations and studies of ESP which appeared in the *Revue Philosophique de la France et de l'Étranger* (Richet, 1884b) and in the *Proceedings of the Society for Psychical Research* (Richet, 1888b, 1889), which I will comment on below.

In 1892, he attended séances in Milan with the Italian medium Eusapia Palladino (1854-1918) that opened his mind to the possibility of physical paranormal phenomena (Richet, 1893). In later years he observed Leonora Piper (1857–1950), Marthe Béraud, Franek Kluski (1873-1943), Stephan Ossowiecki (1877-1944), and other mediums.

General Ideas About Psychical Research

In addition to the work summarized below, Richet promoted the development of psychical research in other ways. In France he popularized the topic in prestigious publications such as the *Revue Philosophique de la France et de l'Étranger* (Richet, 1884b, 1888a), an important intellectual review, the pages of which were open to psychical research (Alvarado & Evrard, 2013). Furthermore, he supported important French psychical research initiatives. Richet was one of the founders of the *Annales des Sciences Psychiques*, which started publication in 1891, as well as a supporter of the Institut Métapsychique International from its founding in 1919 to his death. Richet also used his scientific and social prominence to help writers, as can be seen in several prefaces he wrote for books that dealt with psychic topics (e.g., Richet, 1891).

As mentioned previously, Richet also did much to ensure that psychical research was included in the international congresses of psychology. According to an 1892 entry in the journal of philosopher and SPR president Henry Sidgwick (1838-1900), "The ingenious Richet designed to bring the SPR to glory at this Congress" (Sidgwick & Sidgwick, 1906, p. 515). Furthermore, on these occasions, Richet discussed psychical research in positive ways. Presenting at the 1889 Congress, he stated that it was a simple task to dismiss extraordinary facts, but it was not the role of science to do so. He told his audience: "What is extraordinary today will be part of tomorrow's common science" (Richet, 1890, p. 33). He continued this trend in later congresses (Richet, 1892, 1906; see Chapter 4).

All of this, as well as his scientific and social prestige, led to Richet's election as President of the Society for Psychical Research in 1905. In his Presidential Address (Richet, 1905b) he made an effort to popularize the term "métapsychique" (metapsychics), a process that he continued in later years (e.g., Richet, 1922). In his address, and in later publications, Richet mentioned two different types of phenomena, subjective (mental), and objective (physical) manifestations. As he did in other later writings, Richet argued that more research was needed, and stressed the fact that metapsychics was a field "where everything is unknown" (Richet, 1905b, p. 28).

From the beginning of his career in psychical research, Richet recognized the existing resistance to psychic phenomena. He stated that there were "improbable facts; but their improbability is entirely relative; in the sense that none of them contradict the known facts acquired by science" (Richet, 1884b, p. 615). Later he expanded this argument by saying:

> Astronomy and physiology, physics and mathematics, chemistry and zoology, need not be afraid. They are intangible, and nothing will injure the imposing assemblage of incontestable facts which constitute them. But notions, hitherto unknown, may be introduced, which, without casting doubts upon pristine truths, may cause new ones to enter their domain, and change, or even upset, our established notions of things.

The facts may be unforeseen, but they will never be contradictory (Richet, 1903/1905c, p. xvii).

While Richet was well aware of the resistance of many scientists to metapsychics and its phenomena, he believed that they should consider that scientific theories are not definitive and should not be used to deny facts; that psychic phenomena do not contradict established facts; and that facts should take precedence over ideas and tradition, while metapsychics presents many facts impossible to deny (Richet, n.d.a, pp. 29–30).

His physiological approach was evident in his life-long concern for psychical research, which he considered to be part of physiology. "Metapsychic phenomena," he wrote, "are at the borders of physiology itself, but of very uncertain physiology" (Richet, 1905b, p. 31). Richet referred to the mental phenomena of acquisition of information as "a new chapter in physiology" (Richet, 1923a, p. 496). He believed the phenomena of Palladino were part of the "domain of experimental physiology" (Richet, 1932, p. 154).

Although Richet wrote much about psychic phenomena, perhaps his best and most influential work was his *Traité de Métapsychique*, published in 1922 (its second edition was translated into English as *Thirty Years of Psychical Research*, Richet, 1923b). The book, a detailed overview of psychical research, was divided into four sections to cover metapsychics in general, subjective and objective metapsychics, and a conclusion (For more about this book see Chapter 5). Richet stated in the book that there was good evidence to believe in the reality of cryptesthesia (supernormal knowledge), telekinesis and materializations.

This positive outlook also appeared in later works. In his autobiography, *Souvenirs d'un Physiologiste* Richet (1933b) stated that metapsychics was the science of the future (on this autobiography see Chapter 2). He also believed metapsychics would enlarge humanity's outlook (Richet, 1933a). Finally, in a book published in the year of his death, Richet wrote that the inhabitual, or psychic phenomena "will have a place in science … A new moral ideal will be the consequence, but not the basis of this new science" (Richet, 1935, p. 103).

ESP

The best known of Richet's earlier papers, and an early classic of psychical research, was a paper called "La Suggestion Mentale et le Calcul des Probabilités" (Richet, 1884b). The paper included reports of various card-guessing tests as well as of the use of objects and photographs of statues as targets. There were also tests in which table turning and a dowsing rod were used to elicit motor responses. But the paper is better known for the use of statistical analyses to evaluate guessing (For more details see Chapter 2).

Commenting on claims about the effects of medicines and drugs on individuals blind to their nature (Bourru & Burot, 1886), Richet discussed methodological issues, such as the importance of participants and experimenters being blind as to the nature of the substances, and the use of a low number of substances that would allow for a statistical evaluation of the results (Richet, 1886a).

Richet (1888b) reported other tests of clairvoyance and attempts to induce trance at a distance with various participants, and particularly, with four women: Léonie, Alice, Eugénie, and Héléna. The first one, Léonie Leboulanger (born 1837), was the famous hypnotic virtuosa studied by the student of dissociation Pierre Janet (1859-1947), both in tests of the induction of trance at a distance (Janet, 1886) and in observations of secondary personalities under hypnosis (Janet, 1889).[2] In this report, Richet emphasized the importance of experimental demonstration and expressed hope that the day would come when alternative explanations for the research results could be discarded with confidence. This included fraud by the participants and the involuntary expectations of experimenters.

An example of this activity is a description of a place at a distance by Alice (Richet, 1888b, p, 154). The target was a country house owned by Mme. A., who was present, but remained silent. Richet himself knew nothing about this place. He asked Alice for a description, and she described correctly a garden with railings, with no trees in front, a stone stair with four steps, a clock above the fireplace, and on the right and left of the clock two angels. All the details, Richet wrote, were correct except for the fact that the two figures were actually goats.

While Richet could not explain his results, he wrote: "I would say that in some psychic states, among a small number of subjects, there is a *faculty of knowledge* which differs absolutely from our faculties of ordinary knowledge" (Richet, 1888b, p. 166).

In another report, Richet described tests with Léonie using playing cards put inside envelopes. Richet hypnotized her and asked her second personalities to take the tests. He wrote:

> She spent two months and a half in my house. ... As I could keep her entranced for a long time without injury to her—generally during the night—I have repeatedly sat by her side from 8:00 p.m. till 6:00 a.m. For it was not in the earliest moments of her trance that she could tell the cards under the envelope, but after long and apparently very laborious endeavor (Richet, 1889, p. 68).

Léonie held the envelopes between her hands and took hours to guess the cards. Richet noted that clairvoyance was an inconsistent phenomenon and that Léonie had particular success with cards that had kings, queens and aces. As an aside, Richet said in a footnote that he suspected Léonie of trickery when she was left alone with the envelopes that had cards inside, something that was not part of the usual testing procedure. This fraudulent activity, he was quick to say, came from her secondary personalities (Richet, 1889, p. 77).

On one occasion, while Léonie was trying to guess a diagram inside an envelope, Richet suddenly asked her about his laboratory assistant Langlois:

"He has burnt himself," Leonie replied. "Good," I said, "and where has he burnt himself?" "On the left hand. It is not fire: it is—I don't know its name. Why does he not take care when he pours it out?" "Of what colour," I asked, "is the stuff which he pours out?" "It is not red, it is brown; he has hurt himself very much—the skin puffed up directly" (Richet, 1889, p. 69).

This turned out to be correct. Earlier in the day Langlois accidentally poured bromine on his left hand and a blister had formed.

During the 1920s, Richet also had the opportunity to test Polish psychic Stefan Ossowiecki. In one test, designed to see if the psychic could perceive the contents of a sealed envelope, Richet asked his friend, the famous actress Sarah Bernhardt (1844–1923), to send him a letter that he could use to test Ossowiecki. The psychic was handed the letter, which Richet had not opened, and was told who had sent it. It contained a short message saying: "Life seems good to us, because we know it to be ephemeral!" The reading went for about two hours, and then the psychic said the word "life" several times, adding that Bernhardt signed the letter with vertical strokes (which was correct). Then he said the following: "Life seems humble because there is nothing but hatred; this is so French a word that I cannot say it, it is a word of eight letters, note of exclamation" (Richet, n.d.b, p. 154). The word ephemeral has eight letters in French, and Ossowiecki was not familiar with it.

While Richet valued the experiment above other approaches, he also paid attention to the study of spontaneous experiences, as can be seen in his *Traité*. In his preface to the French abridged edition of Gurney,

Myers and Podmore's *Phantasms of the Living* (1886) he stated that he started reading the accounts of spontaneous telepathy with some incredulity, but that he gradually became convinced that "most of the stories were honest" and that "the multiple precautions necessary to ensure accurate exact testimonies, the authenticity of facts, had been taken, and that, as extraordinary as the conclusion was, one cannot not refuse to admit it" (Richet, 1891, p. viii).

Richet also put on record some spontaneous ESP experiences, including a few about his own family. In one of these, he visited his maternal grandfather, Charles Renouard, in his country house; the old man was indisposed but otherwise had been in general good health. A few days later, Richet's wife dreamed she saw the grandfather very ill in bed, and his wife by his side.

A subsequent telegram informed Richet of the sudden death of the grandfather due to heart problems. Richet now learned that his grandmother had been present at the country house, a fact known neither to himself nor to his wife (Richet, 1888b, pp. 162–163).

In another instance Richet himself had an experience:

> One evening, during the winter of 1899, I was at home in my library. My wife had that night been to the Opera with my daughter Louise. Suddenly, about half-past ten o'clock, I imagined, for the first time in my life and without there being the slightest odour of smoke in the room, that the Opera was on fire. So powerful was my conviction, that I wrote on a piece of paper the words: Feu! Feu! A few minutes afterwards ... I wrote: Att. (i.e. attention). Then, without feeling at all disturbed, I resumed my work. About midnight, on the return of my wife

and daughter, I immediately asked them if there has been a fire ... "No," answered my wife, "there has not been a fire, only a false alarm ... Between the acts there was a rumour of fire and I rushed out to see what it meant ... I was quickly assured there was no danger and the performance continued without a break" ... At the very moment of my writing on the piece of paper the words Feu! Feu! Att., my sister ..., whose rooms on the same floor are separated from mine only by a door, imagines that my room was on fire. She goes to the door between the two apartments, and, when on the point of turning the handle ... she stops, saying to herself: "No, after all, I won't disturb my brother for such a trifle!" (Richet, n.d.b, pp. 60–61).

In later years, Richet collected cases of telepathy and presentiments, among World War One soldiers, some of which were published (de Vesme, 1919; Richet, 1917). He also authored a book about premonitions. About dreams of the future he observed: "In general, but with many exceptions, people who have prophetic dreams will remember them with clarity and can recount all their details" (Richet, n.d.a, p. 13).

Mental Mediums

Leonora Piper was one of the mediums with whom Richet held séances. Richet's comments about sittings, which he had in 1889 in England, appeared in a report about the medium by Leaf (1890, pp. 618–620). But he was not impressed by most of the information presented by her (see Appendix A.).

He also wrote briefly, about a family incident, of what he considered lucidity with the medium Rosalie Thompson (born 1868). The medium held a watch belonging to Richet's son, George (1878-1967), and said "Three generations mixed." The watch had been given by George's maternal grandfather to his son. After the son's death, another member of the family inherited it and it eventually passed into George's hands (Richet, 1922, p. 192).

Richet also wrote about powers of personation: that is, the medium's subconscious abilities to simulate spirit personalities. He stated: "In reality all the intelligent manifestations attributed to the spirits are due to an individual that is unconscious and active at the same time" (Richet, 1884b, p. 650). In this view, the medium's intelligence, memory and will functioned without her conscious awareness (On this issue see Chapter 6).

In a paper published two years later, Richet discussed unconscious movements involved in table-tilting, which convinced him that mediums had a hidden train of thought (that is, that there was a "simultaneous existence of another collateral thought" (Richet, 1886c, p. 87). As he had argued before (Richet, 1884b), he stated that mediums could present "a series of ideas completely different from the series of ideas of the conscious personage, who ignores all that takes place in its unconscious" (Richet, 1886c, p. 93).

Physical Mediums

Richet took part in the famous Milan séances with Eusapia Palladino, which brought together scholars and scientists such as Alexander Aksakof (1832–1903), Carl du Prel

(1839–1899), Giovanni Schiaparelli (1835–1910), and others (Aksakof et al., 1893). Their view was that the phenomena they witnessed—including the anomalous movement of objects and the appearance of ghostly hands—were genuinely paranormal. Richet declined to add his name to their declaration, conflicted about what he had seen. In one instance, at a time when he was sure that both of Palladino's hands were properly controlled, the medium asked the sitters to look above her head, where Richet saw a "hand that opened and closed" (Richet, 1893, p. 20). The hand, he noted, looked different from the medium's. On another occasion, he saw a hand "surrounded by a white veil or by a white light" (Richet, 1893, p. 22) (although he added that he was uncertain about this observation). But, although he found it hard to attribute everything he had witnessed to trickery, he remained uncertain. In his words, "the formal, undeniable proof, that this is not a fraud on the part of Eusapia and an illusion on our part, this formal proof is lacking" (Richet, 1893, p. 31).

However, in later séances conducted in France, Richet became certain that the phenomena witnessed there were real (Lodge, 1894; Richet, 1895).

> On one occasion, among others, I was holding in one hand the two hands of Eusapia; I raised my other hand in the air, very high; then the hand that is in the air is grabbed vigorously by a hand which grasps two fingers, pulls them strongly and, after having pulled them, gives me on the back of that same hand a rather strong tap that everyone hears (Richet, 1895, p. 70).

Perhaps the most controversial episodes in Richet's career were the materialization séances he conducted with Marthe Béraud (Richet, 1905a; see also Chapter 2). These took place in Algiers, where a private circle had been witnessing the appearance of figures, notably a bearded man, referred to as Bien Boa (B.B.) wearing what looked like a metallic helmet under loose white drapery. On one occasion, Richet wrote:

> I saw as it were a white luminous ball floating over the ground; then, rising straight upwards, very rapidly, as though issuing from a trap door, appeared B.B. He appeared to me to be of no great height; he had a drapery and, I think, something like a caftan with a girdle at the waist ... But the coming out was sudden, and the luminous spot on the floor preceded the appearance of B.B. outside the curtain, and he raised himself straight up *(developing his form rapidly in a straight line)* (Richet, 1905a, p. 273).

This and other observations—such as when the figure disappeared into the ground—convinced Richet that they were real materializations, although he also spoke of puzzling inconsistencies in the photographs.

Soon after he published an account of the séances, controversies erupted (Le Maléfan, 2002; see also Chapter 2). There were claims that the medium had admitted fraud—that a person said he had played the part of the materialization, and that the figure's disappearances in the floor were facilitated by a trap door—although Richet testified that he had closely examined the building, and that there was no trap door. The episode somewhat damaged Richet's reputation. Nonetheless, in later years, Richet maintained his conviction that the critiques could not explain all that he had witnessed (Richet, 1922, pp. 646–648). While

Béraud is usually discussed in terms of Richet's formal report (Richet, 1905a), some of his observations on the medium published in *Traité* are rarely mentioned. These were recorded in notes he made in 1906, during an incident in which he and a female sitter were alone with the medium in a room, and he was able to observe ectoplasm moving around (see Appendix B.).

Richet attended more séances with Béraud, when she was being studied by other investigators under the name "Eva C" (see Schrenck-Notzing, 1920, pp. 72–74, 77–78). He also sat with the Italian medium Linda Gazzera. In a séance held in darkness, but with the medium's arms and feet controlled, Richet described "a huge chest" twenty-five centimeters from her, beginning to "oscillate and to crack, and to move with such violence that I was afraid it would fall; because it was poorly balanced" (Richet, 1922, p. 552).

There were also seances with many other mediums, among them the Poles Franek Kluski and Jean Guzik (1876-1928) (as recorded by Geley, 1922/1927, pp. 223–257, 286–288). In his notes of a séance with Kluski, Richet mentioned bluish points of light of "approximately three millimeters in diameter, which wandered in the air, sometimes quite far from the medium" (Geley, 1921, p. 176).

Richet hypothesized that there were various phases of materialization. He wrote that the first phase was of something invisible that could move objects and produce other physical effects. Then they become visible, but cloudy. Later still, they have human forms, as they have the extraordinary property of changing form, consistence, and to evolve before our eyes. In a few seconds this nebulous embryo, which exits the body of the medium, becomes a true being (Richet, 1922, p. 784).

Richet identified these effusions as "ectoplasms; that is, sarcodic extensions coming from the human body (of mediums)", similar to the "pseudopodic projections seen on amoebas", and argued that "this ectoplasmic formation at the expense of the anatomo-physiological organism of the medium is now beyond dispute" (Richet, 1922, p. 783). The term 'ectoplasm' subsequently came to be generally applied to this mediumistic phenomenon (see Appendix C.).

The issue of fraud in physical mediumship was not ignored by Richet. He was aware that the extraordinary appearance of the phenomena naturally raised the spectre of fraud, and the presence of trickery was indeed often confirmed with some mediums. But he was skeptical of fraud as a blanket explanation for the phenomena he witnessed, remarking: "When I think of the precautions that we have taken, twenty times, a hundred times, a thousand times, it is unacceptable that we were all twenty times, a hundred times, a thousand times misled" (Richet, 1922, p. 596).

Theoretical Ideas

Throughout his writings, Richet expressed dissatisfaction with the various explanations of psychic phenomena that were being put forward, including the hypothesis of discarnate agency (e.g., Richet, 1905b, 1922). In his *Traité*, he accepted the reality of many phenomena but said that there was not a proper theory to explain them, and placed his hopes in future developments. Nonetheless, Richet presented several speculations over the years. One was the existence of a faculty of cognition that was purely human. In an early paper, he postulated that

ESP messages impinged on the "unconscious faculties of intelligence" (Richet, 1884b, p. 639).

Other speculations were connected to the old idea, developed before Richet, that various concepts of biophysical forces explained psychic phenomena (Alvarado, 2006). Throughout his career Richet speculated on the possibility of unspecified vibrations as a way to explain the mental phenomena of psychical research. In an early statement he speculated about the existence of a force emanating from one person to another "such that the vibration of the thought of an individual influences the vibration of the thought of a nearby individual" (Richet, 1884b, p. 617). He wrote in later years: "The sixth sense is that one which gives us knowledge of a vibration of reality, a vibration which our normal senses are unable to perceive" (Richet, n.d.b, p. 224).

Regarding physical phenomena, noticing how instruments can measure light, electricity and temperature from the human body, Richet asked if it was "unreasonable to assume that the projection of light, heat, and electricity could be accompanied by a mechanical projection of force" (Richet, 1922, p. 597). He continued:

> Materialization is a mechanical projection. We already have the projection of light, heat, and electricity. It is not going very far to consider as possible other projections ... a projection of mechanical force. The memorable demonstrations of Einstein come to establish at what point mechanical energy approximates luminous energy (Richet, 1922, pp. 597–598).[3]

On the subject of materializations, Richet believed the most rational and straightforward explanation was that of a projection outside of the body "of a material substance capable of organizing [itself]" (Richet, 1922, pp. 784–785). But he admitted that this idea was not so simple, requiring as it did a new physiology, physics, and chemistry.

In his discussions of premonitions, Richet referred to the possibility that apparent knowledge of the future was due to "the imperfect and fragmentary knowledge of the present" acquired by psychic means (Richet, n.d.a, p. 197). That is, some premonitions are not necessarily about the future, but may be produced by psychic impressions of contemporary events leading to the future.

Survival of Death

Richet was outspoken about his doubts regarding the evidence for survival of death. For him, the alternative explanations of personation and cryptesthesia were serious contenders. He wrote of cryptesthesia: "This new faculty of the mind is much simpler than survival, because survival supposes incredible amount of facts, unheard of, which collide in front of all accepted physiological truths, which are contrary also to logic, and which warns us that what is born must die." (Richet, 1922, p. 261).

He added his conviction that the power of the human mind to "group its recollections and knowledge, metapsychic or not … around some or other imaginary personality, is not a hypothesis: it is a fact. And then it is the simplest assumption" (Richet, 1922, p. 261).

This attitude about personation was informed by his earlier tests in the use of hypnosis to induce personality changes (Richet, 1883). In a section at the beginning of his *Traité*, about the frontiers between psychological and metapsychic phenomena, he discussed the creative powers of the subconscious mind to simulate spirit personalities with mediums (see Chapter 6). He believed that before accepting metapsychic manifestations, we should exhaust all possible psychological explanations, such as personation, unconscious memory, and elaboration (creative construction of stories). Like others before him (e.g., Flournoy, 1900), Richet used the idea of these talents to object to explanations of mediumship and other phenomena in terms of ideas of discarnate action.

Nonetheless, Richet seems to have had doubts about the explanatory powers of his ideas. Oliver Lodge (1851–1940) wrote that in private communications Richet "confessed to me that he was sometimes nearly bowled over by the evidence; but, on the whole, he adhered to his lifelong conviction of the materialistic aspect of the universe" (Lodge, 1936, p. 4). Furthermore, Richet was sometimes impressed by some manifestations. He wrote:

> There are ... a few cases, rare no doubt, but of an importance that I do not disguise, in which there are, or seem to be, intelligent and reasoned intentions, forces, and acts of will apparent in the phenomena produced, and these have all the characteristics of being due to extraneous action. I allude more especially to the visions of young children when dying. These facts would be exceedingly curious and noteworthy if they stood alone, but *they do*

not stand alone. I have mentioned two precisely similar; and their similarity, or rather their identity, is so definite that it is impossible to admit chance or imaginative fancy as their cause. Such facts are highly important. They are much more explicable by the spirit-hypothesis than by that of cryptaesthesia. It even seems to me that among all the facts adduced to prove survival, these are the most disconcerting; I have, therefore, been scrupulous to mention them. Nevertheless, despite their spiritoid appearance, these facts are not sufficient to make me infer that the consciousness of deceased persons appears as a phantom at the death of a relative (Richet, 1924, p. 276).

Richet seems to have changed in his thinking in later years. In his book *La Grande Espérance*, and later elsewhere, he wrote that metapsychics was the great hope for humankind, illuminating its future (Richet, 1933b, 1935). Oliver Lodge and Ernesto Bozzano (1862-1943), both strong believers in survival of death, were told by Richet that he was coming round to their way of thinking (Bubb, 1936; Lodge, 1936). Richet wrote to Lodge:

> I will publish a book entitled *La Grande Espérance*. And, without being resolutely spiritist in the sense of Conan Doyle and Allan Kardec, I gradually get closer to your ideas. I say to you—which is absolutely true— that your deep and scientific conviction had great influence, a very great influence (Lodge, 1936, p. 4).

However, this letter does not completely support the idea, promoted by some authors, that Richet accepted survival of death as the explanation for some psychic phenomena at the end of his life (e.g., Magalhães, 2007). It is possible that these last two books showed a less materialistic aspect of Richet, but that is a far cry from saying that he became convinced of survival. Furthermore, in *La Grande Espérance* Richet did not declare belief in spirit agency but rather argued that there were problems with both human and spirit-based explanations. In both cases, he wrote, "we face monstrous improbabilities; we swim in the inhabitual, the miraculous, the prodigious" (Richet, 1933a, p. 289).

Recent Scholarship About Richet's Psychical Research

Interest in Richet has grown in recent decades. One of the more important studies—and one not specifically concerned with psychical research—is Wolf's (1993) book-length biography, the only one that exists in English. Wolf focused on Richet's physiological work, but also covered interesting details about his life and non-physiological endeavors. Others have discussed Richet in relation to his literary work and modernist approach (Carroy, 2004), also as an example of creativity in research (Estingoy, 2003), of the social role of physicians (Schneider, 2001), and various other aspects (van Wijland, 2015).

Historians who discuss French psychical research— among them Brower (2010), Lachapelle (2011), Monroe (2008), and Plas (2000)—have explored aspects of Richet's psychical research in the context of dissatisfaction with current psychology, and the interplay between subjective and objective ways to knowledge. All of them have placed him as a central figure in French psychology and psychical research, as has Evrard (2016; see also Evrard, Gumpper, Beauvis, & Alvarado, in press). Outside of academic history, Magalhães (2007) has provided an overview of aspects of Richet's involvement with psychic phenomena from the point of view of the reality of psychic phenomena and of survival of death. There has also been a study of the controversies involving Richet's study of the materializations of Marthe Béraud (Le Maléfan, 2002), and I have published discussions of various aspects of Richet's work (reprinted in Chapters 2–6).

CHAPTER 2

Richet's Metapsychic Autobiography

~

P ast autobiographies of researchers in—and students of—parapsychology (e.g., Lodge, 1931, Chapters 22–24; Rhine, 1983), as well as recollections compiled more recently (Pilkington, 2013) have been of particular value to understand the life and work of various individuals. Following on this interest, I present here a reprint and a translation of an autobiographical account authored by Richet. One of the purposes of this chapter is to present information about Richet's interest in psychic phenomena via his own, admittedly brief, account. It is my impression that most contemporary workers in parapsychology, and other readers, although aware of Richet's existence, know little about his actual work. Being short, the excerpt presented below may present a more personal perspective of Richet's psychic work.

The reprint of the excerpt is also an opportunity to give Richet a voice never heard before in English, since the excerpt in question was originally published in French. Furthermore, I hope to use the example of Richet's essay to highlight the problems of autobiographies in the study of parapsychology's past.

Richet's Autobiographical Comments

The essay reprinted here was taken from Richet's *Souvenirs d'un Physiologiste* (1933), an autobiographical account of various aspects of his career, but with little information about his family. The book was described by a reviewer as the product of a "long and passionate experience of life" (Pierret, 1935).

He stated in the first chapter that it was pleasurable for him to recollect "the persons as well as the uncertainties, the obstacles, the satisfactions and disappointments that have crossed my path" (Richet, 1933, p. 7). Richet also expressed hope that his recollections could show young people the ways by which a physiologist could establish new facts.

The book has 20 chapters full of interesting anecdotes of Richet's early, middle, and later life, anecdotes touching on many personalities and incidents, and on research and publications that illustrate his interests in many topics. An example of one of them is Richet's statement that during a cruise he read his play *Circé* to Albert I, Prince of Monaco (1848–1922), who had it presented in Monte Carlo. The lead role went to the famous Sarah Bernhardt (1844–1923), whom Richet knew.

Some other topics discussed by Richet were his initial research on anaphylaxis with Paul Portier (1866–1962), his work with serotherapy, his passion for medical and physiological bibliography, female workers in his laboratory, his editorship of the *Revue Scientifique*, his *Dictionnaire de Physiologie*, his anti-war activities, and his interest in airplanes and their development.

In addition, Richet commented on the scientific enterprise. In one chapter he argued that science does not advance if it is not audacious. He wrote: "We must construct the most incredible, the most reckless hypotheses, even if they contradict the most classic universally accepted facts" (p. 128).

Psychic phenomena were commented on in the last chapter (pp. 147–156). A translation of this section follows.

Richet's Essay

A close relationship perhaps may be found between the occultist psychophysiology, which I have cultivated with zeal, and the normal psychophysiology that I have taught with no less zeal. Because I give here my recollections as a physiologist, I am forced to speak a little about the so-called occult sciences, nearly taboo, which have taken a large part of my time, which I have at heart, and which inspire my old soul with a great hope.[1]

My interest had quite a singular beginning. Being very young then, a student of philosophy at the Lycée Condorcet, I had the opportunity to attend a session of somnambulism and hypnotism given by a magnetizer named Cannelle who put his very pretty wife to sleep and demonstrated that she had become insensitive.

I was very struck by this experience and, one day, I put one of the friends of my sister to sleep. (I was but sixteen years old.) After a few passes she closed her eyes, and was unable to open them. My sister and I were extremely upset, thinking that our parents would scold us. We did not talk then, but I promised to myself to resume, when the opportunity arose, this experience, which had amazed me.

Three years later ... I magnetized a few patients. At the time I had a very distinct power for hypnotizing but after nearly fifty years I have, it seems, lost all that power.[2]

Here is a memory that is also present in my mind as if the thing had happened yesterday (although it would seem it is from sixty years ago). There was, in a room, quite a young girl, of 16 years of age, barely sick, whom I put to sleep easily. I tried to have one of my friends witness this, a young American, a medical student like me. He had never [before] come to the Hôtel-Dieu.[3] I put little Adrienne to sleep and, once she was asleep, I wanted to examine whether she would show some phenomena of lucidity. So I asked her to tell me the name of the friend who was with me, which made her laugh because she did not know him at all. "Look," I told her, "read his name." I did not write the name, of course. I limited myself to thinking about it, and she said "H. E. and then a letter I do not see, then R. and N." My friend was called Hearn.

Alas! Alas! I refused to admit the reality of this admirable experience. She had to convince me that lucidity exists. But I took no account of it. It is rather sad that we do not see except that which we are accustomed to see and that we want to see.

My 1872 blindness gives me a great understanding for those who, today, despite clear evidence of lucidity that we have presented, continue to deny it stubbornly.

I doubted lucidity; I had no doubt of anything from hypnotism, and I would have continued my research at the Hôtel-Dieu if my teacher and friend Henri Liouville,[4] who was then head of the clinic at Behier, had not formally prohibited it. I protested strongly, but in vain. So I had to wait for more favorable conditions.

They were not long in coming. I entered the service as an intern of Professor Léon Le Fort[5] at the Beaujon Hospital. There I was almost my own teacher, in the service of women who were mildly ill patients, and then, for six months, in follow-up visits every night, I put one or two patients to sleep, sometimes more. Hypnotic sleep was easily achieved, but I was not concerned about lucidity and occultism, a phenomenon I did not *want* to believe, as I was trying only to obtain a hypnotic state. The rooms of the Beaujon Hospital had become like a court of miracles. I could do many experiments that showed me the absolute reality of induced somnambulism.

I wished then to publish these facts that seemed to me to be new and remarkable.

At that time, in 1875, we looked with scorn and indignation on all that was written about somnambulism. In his great encyclopedic dictionary of the medical sciences, Dechambre presented a paper about somnambulism and it ended with these words printed in large letters, the largest in the whole book: "Ultimately animal magnetism does not exist."[6]

In my paper, I demonstrated that it does exist. When I spoke of my project to my father, he told me these simple words; "You therefore want to waste yourself? Is it that one is wasted telling the truth? You are right," he responded after a long silence, "do as you will."

Very liberally, Professor Charles Robin accepted the publication of my paper in his journal.[7] A few months after, a paper by the great physiologist Heidenhain confirmed what I had said. And then the experiences of Charcot, partially inspired by me (then an intern at the Salpetrière), and especially by Ruault, ... [in training with] Charcot, and a powerful hypnotist.[8]

So at the same time when I was pursuing my physiological chemistry experiments, I studied somnambulism.[9] I had some rather remarkable subjects, and then I made experiments (which had some impact) on personality changes, phenomena which I called—although the name is a little barbaric—the objectification of types. Somnambulists, when asleep, forget everything becoming the character they are induced to be and this change is so deep that we are always amazed. I said to Alice, "You are an old woman. Tell me what you feel? ..." "What! Speak louder, I am hard of hearing." Sometimes the change is to something that is funny. Having hypnotized my dear friend Henry Ferrari, and having changed him into a parrot, I noticed that he was a little uneasy; "Did I eat," he asked, "the grain that is in my cage?" These experiences are recounted with details in a long paper, which Th. Ribot published in his *Revue Philosophique.*[10]

I was conducting my research, when I received a visit from a prominent Russian psychologist, Aksakoff, who reproached me for not knowing the facts of spiritualism, facts made much more interesting, according to him, than all of somnambulism. "To see one of these facts," I said, "I would go to the end of the world." He only smiled. But some time later he wrote to me: "It is not about going to the end of the world, but only to Milan."[11]

I went to Milan.

There I saw a quite extraordinary woman, Eusapia Paladino. I cannot speak about her without a real recognition of her importance to me, as it is mainly to her that I owe becoming so interested in the occult sciences.

In Milan, with Lombroso, Schiaparelli, Gerosa, and mainly Finzi, I saw some remarkable things which did not bring me absolute conviction, but which made me lean strongly toward acceptance of occult facts.[12]

I decided to continue to seek new experiences with Eusapia and since that time—that is after almost forty-five years—I have conducted an uninterrupted series of studies on occultism.[13]

First, I had the chance to experiment on one of my charming and loyal friends, Gaston Fournier, who was a remarkable medium.

The decisive experiment I did with him was the following. A table was prepared so that movements were indicated by an electric bell. The alphabet, placed at the end of the room, was in semi-darkness. Gaston had his back turned. He put his hands on the table and made it move, in accordance with the letters over which we silently passed a pencil. We then got precise answers that had no great interest by themselves, except to show Gaston's lucidity because he could not see the letters of the alphabet. I called this the test of the *hidden alphabet*.[14]

At that time a psychic society was founded in England, which soon became, thanks to the eminent persons who founded it, the most important psychological society in the world. I came into close relations with the founding scholars of the new society: Gurney, Myers, Sedgwick [sic], Oliver Lodge. It was also at this time that their admirable book was published, *Phantasms of the Living*, which is like the breviary of serious occultism.[15]

Eusapia exhibited some very curious phenomena. But that did not satisfy me. I decided to begin again. So I had her come to a tiny Mediterranean island that I owned, on which I was the only inhabitant.

Aided by my learned friend Julien Ochorowicz, I devoted three months to experimenting with Eusapia.[16] Every two days we spent several hours (overnight) studying the strange phenomena that Eusapia presented.

This woman, great and prodigious, was also scrutinized elsewhere in the most penetrating way by leading scholars, the most learned Italian physiologists, by Bottazzi, Foa, Herlitzka, Fieeding [sic], Myers, Schrenck-Notzing, Albert de Rochas, Flammarion, d'Arnsoval, Curie, Mme. Curie, Courtier, etc., etc.[17]

I do not believe that any medium has ever been subjected to such severe surveillance, which was also repeated. However, she was accused of fraud, and Myers was tempted to believe in fraud. While at home one day in Paris, after a brilliant experience, I said to Myers: "This time are you sure of the reality of the phenomena, you will never look back on this belief?" And he swore it to me.[18]

I had close ties with Fr. Myers for whom I professed as much affection as admiration. We made many psychological trips to see renowned mediums in Zwickau (Saxony), in Rome, in Kalmar, Sweden, but I cannot relate them here ...[19]

It has often been said that I was deceived and an ineradicable legend of the mystification that I was subjected to in Algiers was formed.[20]

Here is exactly what happened: at General Noël's, commander of the artillery of Algiers, there were wonderful seances that took place in a small locked room. A red light lit up the room and allowed all of us to see well. We were six people. The room was not very big; rather it was a square of about 5 meters wide. Therefore it was physically impossible for someone to come in without being seen by any of us.

However, the general had a coach driver who boldly stole the general's horses' oats in order to resell them. The general dismissed him. The thief A ... wanted revenge, and he claimed that he had played the phantom. Unfortunately he found reporters, a medical doctor, and a theater director, who believed the words of this scoundrel. A ... appeared on stage waving a cloth, as in the Cloches de Corneville [a French operetta].

That is all. Will I be believed when I say that this is not serious?

I wanted to give a name to this new science. As I had been chosen for president of the *Society for Psychical Research*, in the presidential address that I presented in 1885 [sic] I named it metapsychic science, without knowing that elsewhere some months before, in a small Polish pamphlet, the Polish psychologist Mr. Lutosławski had proposed the same term.[21]

The word metapsychic has had a rapid acceptance, which I find extraordinary, and it is commonly used and understood.[22]

I wrote a big book [which] I called *Traité de Métapsychique*. This book has been translated into English, Spanish, and German. I analyzed and discussed the occult sciences according to the strict discipline of classical science. I give here my main conclusions.

1. There is a mental metapsychics, that is to say, the phenomena of lucidity, premonition, monition, and telepathy. Human intelligence can know realities that are unknown to the senses.

2. There are phenomena of telekinesis, that is to say movement of objects at a distance. In other words, there is a mechanical metapsychics. It is as if, at times, some forms may come out from the organism (forms I have called ectoplasms); and this ectoplasm can be the basis of phantoms [On the term ectoplasm see Appendix C.]

This beautiful new science—even though it is still embryonic and so can barely be called a science—is the science of the unusual. It starts with the unshakable experiments of William Crookes;[23] it continues with the research of Flammarion, Myers, Schrenck-Notzing, of Ochorowicz, and with that of my famous and dear friend Sir Oliver Lodge. I cannot state here all my admiration for these brave, shrewd, prudent men, who have not hesitated to compromise by maintaining unpopular views, facing the dismissive sarcasm of an ignorant and malicious public. Alas! Almost all have preceded me in the great journey toward what they believed to be survival. My friend Sir Oliver Lodge happily bravely continues his apostolate in spiritualism.

I have known many mediums. With some I have experimented only once or twice, with Eglinton, with Slade, with Mrs. Piper,[24] but, as interesting as the observations I made about these great mediums are, I do not have to talk about them here, because I maintain that an opinion cannot be formed from two or three seances.

I have experimented often with Stephan Ossovietzki [*sic*].[25]

If Eusapia is the type of medium who produces physical effects, Stephan is the type of medium who produces mental metapsychics. *His lucidity is dazzling.* I challenge a man of good faith, who experiments with Stephan, not to be convinced that the intellect can know about realities that the senses have not perceived.

It is quite interesting to note that Stephan has no telekinesis effects and, on the other hand, Eusapia has no phenomena of lucidity.[26]

I have often been accused of being a spiritist, that is to say of believing that deceased individuals can communicate their thoughts and memories to mediums, and sometimes reappear and revive, preserving all the materiality of their old earthly life. In truth, I cannot accept the reality of those reports, but I must admit that some strange phenomena do happen that are absolutely inexplicable by the meager data of current science.[27] It is, therefore, appropriate to go beyond and look for the laws of the unusual, because *the unusual exists.* Metapsychics is still in a beginning stage, but I am convinced that it is the science of the future.

A very generous man, Mr. Jean Meyer, founded an international metapsychic institute where remarkable work has been done in this semi-infernal domain by Geley, Osty, Warcollier, J.-C. Roux, and by some men without prejudice who believe in the superior virtue of science.[28]

In my old age I return to my starting point. While young I worshiped the science of life and, in my final days, I worship this science again. But I understand this in a broader way than when I started. The science of life merges with the science of thought, and I forsee a future of magnificent horizons.[29]

I may be wrong, but the honor of being able to conduct such research gives some value to life.[30]

Concluding Remarks

In his essay, Richet reminds us of many important aspects of his career related to psychical research. Among them are his early hypnosis work; his work with the "hidden alphabet;" studies of Palladino; contact with SPR workers, and his *Traité de Métapsychique*. It is clear that the amount of work invested by Richet showed a deep interest in the topic. In fact he said in the essay that he believed metapsychics was "the science of the future."

While Richet's outline of his psychical research career is useful, the account is very brief, barely consisting of mentions of topics and incidents with little or no description. While we cannot expect to have a very detailed account in a chapter, my impression is that Richet presents more details in the book about other topics than about metapsychics. Unfortunately this succinctness produces an account with important omissions. For example, Richet does not mention his early—now classic—use of statistics to evaluate what we would refer to today as ESP (Richet, 1884b; see Chapter 3), nor his later writings about chance and the calculation of probability in later years (e.g., Richet, 1888, p. 25–30, 1893b, 1922, pp. 63–68).

The same can be said of his nineteenth century ESP work with various individuals (Richet, 1888, 1889): among them Léonie Leboulanger (born 1837). In addition to conducting his own tests, Richet was present when Pierre Janet (1886, p. 217) conducted some of his famous tests of induction of trance at a distance with Leboulanger, but he also omitted this information from his essay. Anyone unfamiliar with Richet's publications would not be able to tell that he was a leader of French studies of mental suggestion in general, something that is clear in contemporary (Ochorowicz, 1887) and later accounts (Plas, 2000).

In addition, this account omits various other things. These include the importance Richet gave to specific phenomena he observed with various gifted individuals—Stella, Alice, and Palladino (Richet, 1922, p. 759), and accounts of various spontaneous ESP experiences that were related to him in various ways. The latter includes two veridical experiences related to the death of his maternal grandfather in 1878 (Richet, 1888, pp. 162–163) and his mother in 1884 (Richet 1922, pp. 457–458), which were mentioned in the first chapter.

Such omissions—as well as those regarding speculations about the "sixth sense" in terms of unknown vibrations (Richet, n.d.), involvement in the early psychology congresses (Alvarado, 2017), and in the founding of the *Annales des Sciences Psychiques* (Alvarado & Evrard, 2012)—show the limitations of the essay to provide us with a good view of Richet activities regarding psychic phenomena.

While no autobiography can be complete, the succinctness of essays such as this one cautions us about the use of autobiographical documents as single sources of information to trace someone's life work. Like all human accounts, they are based on personal perspectives about what was important or not, something that may distort the record. Autobiographies, like history in general, are reconstructions of the past, but reconstructions based on one person's perspective and motivations, on their priorities at the moment of ordering the recollections of a lifetime.

The latter is particularly an issue when recollecting controversies. Richet's account of the accusations of fraud surrounding the materialization séances that he had in Algiers (Richet, 1905a; see Note 20) is incomplete. The issue was not *only* that Areski said he faked the phenomena, as Richet simply stated in the essay; there were other issues that went unmentioned, such as the supposed confession of the medium, and the existence of a trap door (For overviews and references, see Brower, 2010, pp. 84–92; Evrard, 2016, pp, 172–199; and Le Maléfan 2002). Regardless of the validity of the critiques—and Richet dealt with them at the time—a modern reader unfamiliar with the situation will find that Richet was very selective in his account of the events.

Such selectivity extends to Richet's gloss of critiques about his best-known work, the *Traité de Métapsychique*. Readers of Richet's autobiographical essay will not realize the differences of opinion that the book elicited. Some of these critiques were negative, not only putting in doubt Richet's conclusions, but also casting doubts over metapsychics as a discipline (Janet, 1923; Piéron, 1922). At the other extreme were the critiques of others, among them Gustave Geley (1922) and Oliver Lodge (1923), who accepted metapsychic phenomena, but took issue with Richet's materialistic ideology, including his doubts about the possibility of discarnate action.

Furthermore, there is the problem of correct recollection of facts, since the whole account is based on memory. A few statements in the essay illustrate the problems with memory reconstruction. For one, there is the mistake of saying that the SPR Presidential Address was presented in 1885, when this took place in 1905 (Richet, 1905b), although this could have been a typographical mistake. More important is the lack of perspective when Richet stated in the essay about Palladino that "it is mainly to her that I owe being so interested in the occult sciences." While there is no question that the seances with the medium had a great impact on him, we cannot forget that, by the time that Richet had his first seances in 1892, he had already shown much interest in psychic phenomena, particularly what we refer today as ESP (Richet, 1884b, 1886, 1888, 1889).

This problem with perspective is also evident with the lack of a chronological sequence of events mentioned in the essay. The reader is not informed about the year, or time period, when Palladino, Piper, and Ossowiecki are mentioned. The same can be said of Richet's *Traité*. Not all readers will know that this was published in 1922.[31]

My intention has not been to criticize Richet. Instead, I believe that all these problems, typical of the writings of others apart from Richet's, alert us to the limitations of autobiographical documents when they are used to understand lives and the history of a field—something that extends to the autobiographies of mediums and psychics (Alvarado, 2011). Nonetheless, when used together with other sources of information they are not only informative, but also illuminating of a time period.

CHAPTER 3

Early Ideas and Tests of Mental Suggestion (1884)

A historian of psychology referred to an 1884 attempt "to make mental suggestion a scientific subject by the use of probability calculations" (Carroy, 2004, p. 226). This was a reference to an article by Richet (1884), and to part of the topic of this chapter.

Considered one of the most important nineteenth century reports of experimental ESP tests, "La Suggestion Mentale et le Calcul des Probabilités" [Mental Suggestion and the Calculation of Probability], appeared in the December 1884 issue of the *Revue Philosophique de la France et de l'Étranger*, a mainstream journal unusually open to discussions of psychic phenomena (Alvarado & Evrard, 2013), among them the well-known attempts to induce trance at a distance by Pierre Janet (1886a, 1886b), and others (e.g., Beaunis, 1886; Dufay, 1888). Richet defined mental suggestion in the paper as the "influence that an individual's thought exerts over a specific sense, without an appreciable exterior phenomenon on our senses, over the thought of a nearby individual" (Richet, 1884, p. 615). The term mental suggestion was widely used in France to mean the active sending of thoughts, images, and other effects including commands to induce trance at a distance (for overviews see Ochorowicz, 1887; Plas, 2000, pp. 87–109).

Richet's paper received both sympathetic (Gurney, 1884) and unsympathetic (Franklin, 1885) contemporary commentaries. Later discussions on the statistical aspects of the paper include those of historians (Hacking, 1988, pp. 438–439) and parapsychologists. Among the latter, J. B. Rhine said that Richet deserved "credit for the first use of the mathematics of chance in evaluating results of telepathy tests" (Rhine, 1947, p. 16). Jahn and Dunne (1987) affirmed that Richet's statistical approach "strongly influenced the subsequent analytical strategies" (p. 41) of parapsychology and other disciplines, a statement that deserves more careful historical study.

In this chapter I briefly discuss Richet's statistical studies and point out other generally neglected contributions presented in his 1884 paper.

Statistical Analyses of Richet's Tests

Richet's analyses of guessing tasks introduced statistical analyses to psychical research. His studies included guessing of such things as playing cards, but also "photographs of paintings, of statues, of antique objects, of scenes, of diverse topics" (Richet, 1884, p. 635). Richet commented that the photographs "certainly strike the imagination in a way that is more powerful than a simple playing card" (p. 635). There were also tests in which hidden objects and letters served as targets, and tests in which motor responses were elicited using the dowsing rod and table turning. Richet concluded:

> The method that I have adopted is that of probabilities; it poses the problem thus: Given an arbitrary designation whose probability is known; does the probability of this designation change by the fact of mental suggestion? To this question our experiments allow us to reply affirmatively: For playing cards, the answer by chance should be 458, and it was 510 with suggestion on 1833 tests. For photographs and pictures, the probable number was 42, and the acquired number was 67 on 218 tests. For experiments with the dowsing rod, the probable number was 18, and the real number was 44 on 98 tests. For experiments called spiritistic, the probable number was 3, but the real number was 17 on 124 tests. The results acquired by the calculation of serial probability are more conclusive still. (Richet, 1884, pp. 668–669)

Regarding the latter, Richet stated: "It is completely implausible that chance, on about 300 experiments, can give me so many times these remarkable series" (Richet, 1884, p. 669). Overall, he concluded that his results were not explained by chance. Paraphrasing Pascal, Richet wrote: *"If it was necessary to opt for the reality or not reality of mental suggestion, I would let luck decide; but I would give two chances to the hypothesis that suggestion exists, and one chance only to the opposite hypothesis"* (Richet, 1884, p. 670, Richet's italics).

Assuming the reality of mental suggestion, Richet queried, would this mean that the phenomena would bring a "new era" to science? Not in his opinion. He believed the phenomenon "changes nothing in our actual knowledge about living or inert matter" (Richet, 1884, p. 671).

Reanalyses of Previous Thought-Transference Experiments

In addition to the statistical analyses of his own data, Richet's work presents an early example of the statistical reanalyses of previously published experimental studies (pp. 633–634). For example, in some trials of thought-transference studies published by the Society for Psychical Research (Barrett et al., 1882) it was found that there were five consecutive hits. Richet argued that there was one chance in 52 to select the proper card from a deck of playing cards. The successful guessing of a second card was associated with a "probability . . . of 1/52 x 1/52 . . . and, in consequence, to state exactly five times the suit of a card, the probability is . . . 1/16.680.235 . . ." (p. 633). This, Richet believed, showed that chance did not account for the results. Regarding other tests in the same report in which eight hits were reported to occur, Richet stated that the probability was "$1/52^8$ = 1/7 164 938 643 456" (p. 634). In Richet's view this was equivalent to selecting the single black ball from the remaining 7,164,938,643,455 white balls in an urn.

Mental Suggestion and the Unconscious

Richet believed that mental suggestion acted on the "unconscious faculties of intelligence" (p. 639). The person receiving the message was not aware of the fact. But such information could manifest through weak unconscious movements. This is what led him to use the dowsing rod and table tilting, as discussed below.

Motor Automatisms

In addition to guessing tasks, Richet used motor automatisms to obtain responses from his participants. He reported tests in which the response was produced through movements produced by table turning. To accomplish this, Richet had the persons on the table (designated as C, D, and E) sitting with their backs to two individuals, who sat on a separate table with a board displaying the alphabet. An electric battery was connected to a bell and to the legs of a table so that when any leg was raised the bell would ring. Two other participants were designated as A and B. The person designated as A moved his finger along the alphabet and, when the bell rang (meaning that one of the table's legs rose), B wrote down the letter where the finger was resting. This took place without the table tilters knowing the identity of the letter. Some "quick and repeated movements indicated that the word or the phrase were finished" (p. 653).

To the surprise of C, D, and E, "the word had a meaning, the phrase had a significance" (p. 653). In some tests someone asked for a specific name or reply. Many responses had letters that were either before or after the correct letter in terms of their position in the alphabet and that had the same number of letters, responses that Richet tried to quantify.

Tests were also done using dowsing rods. In one group of tests, several pictures representing objects, animals, and persons were placed on a table. Someone concentrated on a picture, while another tried to select the picture using the rod and its movements as responses. The rod was also used in other places and for other tasks, such as trying to find objects placed on a shelf in Richet's library.

Features of Mental Suggestion

Richet noticed that the faculty was "very capricious, wandering, uncertain" (p. 616). It manifested "in different degrees with different individuals" (p. 616). Richet referred both to target displacement and declines in the subject's performance. The displacements seemed to be related to consistent confusions of one target for another.

Participants

Good results were obtained with adults "in good health, not hypnotized, nor hypnotizable" (p. 632). Most of his tests were done with "non sensitive persons, such as my friends and myself" (p. 632). Richet tested himself repeatedly. He posited that two participants in his studies, Mlle. B. and Mme H., were "very sensitive to magnetism" (p. 635), meaning that they were hypnotizable. These individuals were said to have obtained in some tests 22 hits out of 54 trials, where mean chance expectation was 10.

Tests performed with table tilting were done with five of Richet's childhood friends. They were described as educated and intelligent, and lacking in mystical tendencies. Two of them, Gaston Fourier and Henri Ferrari, were said to be mediums. While Richet and the others could not cause the table to move, his two friends could. It should be pointed out that both Fournier and Ferrari participated in many of the above-mentioned tests, which Richet said were conducted with non-sensitive persons.

Explanation of Mental Suggestion

Richet said that, regarding the explanation of mental suggestion: "Theory, explanation, is currently quite impossible" (p. 618). Nonetheless, while acknowledging that the process behind such phenomena was an unknown one, he speculated. Richet mentioned the possible existence of a force emitted by an agent, "such that the vibration of the thought of an individual influences the vibration of the thought of a nearby individual" (p. 617).

He further wrote that if a candle could "produce a very clear light at night at 200 meters from us, it seems absurd that at three or four meters of distance cerebral activity shows no action on close-by objects" (p. 668).

Mental Suggestion and Science

From the beginning of the paper Richet let his readers know of the controversial and improbable nature of mental suggestion. He said that the topic at hand was different from the "facts commonly admitted by science" (p. 609). The results of mental suggestion tests are "improbable facts; but their improbability is entirely relative; in the sense that none of them contradicts the known facts, acquired by science" (p. 615).

In addition to warning his readers about the incredible nature of the phenomena, he cautioned them to keep in mind the "insufficience and impotence of current science" (p. 609) both to explain many facts of nature as well as mental suggestion.

Mediums

On a different topic, Richet also discussed mediums in terms of the unconscious mind. "In reality," he wrote, "all the intelligent manifestations attributed to the spirits are due to an individual that is unconscious and active at the same time" (p. 650). But such individual (the medium) was not aware of this.

Richet speculated that these persons were in a state of hemisomnambulism in which part of the brain accomplishes some operations, produces thoughts, and receives perceptions without the awareness of the self. The consciousness of this individual persists in its apparent integrity: all the very complicated operations are accomplished outside of consciousness, without the voluntary conscious self apparently feeling any modification (p. 650).

In this view, a medium was a person showing "partial unconsciousness, a faculty by which part of its intelligence, of her memory, of her will, operates out of consciousness" (pp. 650–651).

Concluding Remarks

Although Richet published several influential discussions throughout his career about mental suggestion, and what he later called lucidity and the sixth sense (e.g., Richet, 1888, 1889, n.d.), his 1884 paper is still considered a classic of early experimental parapsychology. Clearly, Richet had more to offer in this paper than card guessing tests and statistical analyses, the latter being of considerable importance. He presented information about reanalyses, targets, motor responses to targets, features of mental suggestion, and participants' characteristics, and speculated that mental suggestion acted unconsciously, and that it may be related to the emission of unspecified vibrations.

Richet's views of vibrations were consistent with ideas of human radiations to explain ESP, ideas that preceded and that were discussed around the time he was writing (Alvarado, 2006, 2015). Richet continued discussing these ideas in later years. As he wrote in the late 1920s: "The sixth sense is that one which gives us knowledge of a vibration of reality, a vibration which our normal senses are unable to perceive" (Richet, n.d., p. 224).

The involvement of non-conscious levels of the mind in telepathy and mediumship was an idea that started being discussed during the nineteenth century by writers with different conceptions about these hidden levels of the mind. Some had postulated that table-tilters produced the movement with their own hands but without their own awareness (e.g., Chevreul, 1854), and that genuine (and veridical) mediumistic phenomena could take place thanks to unconscious reflex actions of the brain (Rogers, 1853). Earlier in 1884, before

Richet's paper was published, there were discussions in publications of the Society for Psychical Research on both the subconscious aspects of motor automatisms and telepathy (Barrett et al., 1884; Myers, 1884). Richet (1886) himself discussed the topic two years later, but his discussions were never as detailed or attentive to the concept of a self-reflective subconscious mind as those of Myers (1884, 1885).

Richet's paper is not only a testament to his creative talents, but also provides us with a fascinating view of concepts and methodology that were developed further in later years.

CHAPTER 4

Presenting Psychical
Research to Psychology
(1905)

~

Another important aspect of Richet's work was his effort to make psychical research part of psychology. This was a difficult enterprise because, over the years, there were many examples of rejection and critiques of psychical research by psychologists. A prominent one was G. Stanley Hall's (1844–1924) review of the work of the Society for Psychical Research (SPR) in the first volume of the *American Journal of Psychology*, a journal, which he founded. Regarding telepathy, Hall (1887) argued that it lacked "everything approaching proof save to amateurs and speculative psychologists" (p. 146).

Many other psychologists were equally skeptical (e.g., Hansen & Lehmann, 1895; Jastrow, 1889; Troland, 1914) for a variety of reasons, a topic discussed in the literature about the history of the field.[1] However—and this is relevant here—there have also been some defences of psychical research whose authors have taken their arguments to psychological forums. Examples of these include William James' (1842–1910) papers in the American journal *Psychological Review* (e.g., James, 1896; see also Alvarado, 2009), and the efforts of others in various psychology journals such as *L'Année Psychologique* (Maxwell, 1907) and the *Journal of Abnormal Psychology* (Carrington, 1915). Another example that is the topic of this chapter was Richet's efforts at the international congresses of psychology. In this chapter I reprint excerpts from one of Richet's congress presentations in 1905.

Richet and the Psychology Congresses

As seen in previous chapters, by the time Richet published the paper, excerpts of which I am reprinting here, he had already distinguished himself in many ways, including psychical research work. Some of Richet's main efforts to develop psychical research inside psychology were connected to the international congresses of psychology. The main discussions of psychic phenomena in the congresses took place in the meetings held between 1889 and 1900, and, to some extent, in 1905.[2]

The first international congress of psychology took place in Paris in 1889 (Alvarado, 2006; Nicolas & Meunier, 2002). The planning was done by the Société de Psychologie Physiologique, of which Richet was a prominent member. Richet acted as Secretary of the congress and was apparently involved in many aspects of its organization. One of the main ones was the inclusion of psychical research as part of the program. Philosopher Henry Sidgwick (1838–1900), who was then the President of the SPR, documented Richet's actions on behalf of psychical research in an entry of his journal dated March 25, 1892:

> Prof. Richet, our friend and colleague in S.P.R. matters, got up a "Congress of Physiological Psychology" in Paris and asked us to come to it. We came out of simple friendship; but when we arrived we found that the ingenious Richet designed to bring the SPR to glory at this Congress. And this, to some degree, came about" (A. Sidgwick & E.M. Sidgwick, 1906, p. 515).

There was some psychical research in the congress (Alvarado, 2006, 2017), particularly discussions about veridical hallucinations (Statistique des Hallucinations, 1890). Richet said, in a paper presenting an overview of the work discussed at the congress, that the use of the word veridical meant that the hallucinatory experiences were "related to a real fact unknown to the person having the hallucination" (Richet, 1890, p. 33). Referring to the concept of telepathy evident in the work of the SPR (Gurney, Myers & Podmore, 1886), and in the discussions at the congress, Richet argued that such a concept would be "one of the greatest discoveries of the times" (Statistique des Hallucinations, 1890, p. 153).[3]

Topics related to psychical research were also discussed in later congresses, particularly in the 1900 congress held at Paris (Janet, 1901) at which many attendants rebelled against the presence of psychic phenomena in the program (Alvarado, 2017). Richet wrote two papers about the future of psychology for the 1892 and 1905 congresses in which he included the study of psychic phenomena (Richet, 1892, 1906a). Both papers were defences of the importance of psychic phenomena for psychology and calls for more research on the subject, something that was not part of the mainstream in psychology.

Richet's Paper

The paper reprinted below was published in the proceedings of the 1905 congress (De Sanctis, 1906), which took place in Rome, but was not read at the conference. The paper appeared in the congress proceedings (Richet, 1906a) and it was also published in English in the *Annals of Psychical Science* (Richet, 1906b), from which I have taken an excerpt appearing below.

During this same year, Richet published several papers about psychic phenomena such as his famous address as President of the Society for Psychical Research entitled "La Métapsychique" (Richet, 1905b), and articles dealing with xenoglossy and materialization phenomena (Richet, 1905a, 1905c).

Recollecting the earlier congresses, Richet stated that he believed psychology was a field bringing together a variety of approaches. His point in the address was to speculate on the future of psychology. He argued that "when we speak of the Future of Psychology, it must be understood that we refer not to the prediction of events that will happen; but that we counsel a certain general direction to be pursued in our researches, in order to realise important and valuable conquests" (Richet, 1906b, p. 202). He warned us that we should not see any part of science as closed because "it often happens that such or such a scientific question may appear to be completely settled whilst in reality it is only imperfectly understood and destined to undergo entire transformation" (p. 202). Furthermore, he believed that each science could affect another, something particularly true in the case of psychology. In the paper he focused on two areas, "the relations of the mind and the body, in other words, physiological psychology" and "the aspect of psychology known as occult, which I have called *metapsychical,* and which ought to be given a place in classical psychology" (p. 203).

Richet on Occult Psychology

The following is taken from Richet's (1906b, pp. 210–216) paper.

Occult psychology is, in my opinion, the field in which we may expect to meet with the most productive surprises.

To begin with, I should like to rid myself of this troublesome term *occult;* because occult means hidden, secret, unknown. All the sciences began by being occult: there is, therefore, no such thing as occult psychology, and I prefer to use the word *metapsychic,* for which I have a paternal partiality.[4]

It seems to me that we should make a great mistake if we neglected the initial processes of metapsychism; because it is easy to foresee that in a few years it will have conquered for itself a right to the light of day. It will have its methods, its demonstrations, its classical treatises,[5] by means of which it will doubtless, like its predecessors, bar the way to new sciences not yet visible on the horizon.

What occurred in relation to somnambulism should never be forgotten: It had been observed as early as 1780 that a peculiar physiological and psychological condition called animal magnetism or somnambulism can be produced by diverse methods. But official science, in spite of innumerable facts, demonstrations, records, books, and journals, in spite of public opinion—which is sometimes more enlightened than science—refused to admit its reality until 1875. At that time, when I was still a young student, I had the good fortune of being able to prove (and that in a way which to me seems definite) that the phenomenon of induced somnambulism belongs to the class of phenomena, which are indisputable, and classical, so that now no one doubts its reality.[6]

It is possible that a similar reaction may occur with regard to metapsychical phenomena; because some facts are established and others are reported by so many different observers from all parts of the world that it is difficult to suppose that all this is but a colossal illusion, or, if the alternative is preferred, a colossal and universal mystification.

Certainly the numerous observers who tell us of haunted houses, of phantoms, of levitations, of predictions, of healing by the laying on of hands, of transmutations of matter, of *apports,* and other strange manifestations, are not all accurate and attentive observers. They are sometimes more credulous than critical; their faith is stronger than their reasoning power; and they test, rather severely, the patience of those who try to sift out the truth from the medley which is supplied to them. Nevertheless it would be unfair to entirely refuse to credit them, on the pretext that their opinions are not the opinions of official savants. William Crookes, Russel Wallace, Zollner, Lombroso, are not mere ciphers, and I imagine that the greater number of us would be legitimately proud to be as well equipped, scientifically, as the least of these. It is not that I bow to authority or that I wish to re-echo the maxim, which has so often retarded science: *Magister dixit.* But, indeed, neither William Crookes, nor Russel Wallace, nor Zollner, nor Lombroso, deserve to be set aside as unworthy to be included in the narrow circle of real savants.

Professor Wundt, however, is not of this opinion: a few years ago he protested with considerable energy against experiments made with sickly, neurotic patients; miserable experiments, he called them, from which men claim to draw conclusions touching immense, universal nature.[7]

"There are two worlds:" he writes ironically, "a great universal world governed by the laws discovered by Copernicus, Galileo, Newton and Helmholtz and another little world composed of a few fanciful and hysterical young girls, which has reactions of quite a different order. Well! My choice is made, I prefer the great world to the small one."

Professor Wundt might be justified in so expressing himself, if he had succeeded in discovering an actual contradiction between these two worlds; but the learned psychologist may reassure himself. Two true facts do not contradict each other, and, if there appears to be contradiction, it is the result of our ignorance. If phantoms and predictions are proved to be realities, that will in no degree whatsoever diminish the truth of the law of attraction; if telepathy is established, the laws that govern the oscillations of a pendulum will remain the same. Has the discovery of radium, which has added so greatly to our knowledge of the nature of matter, affected in any degree the teachings of chemistry concerning the combinations of iodine and iron?

The little worlds, which Professor Wundt treats with aristocratic disdain, are not to be so much disdained. A fragment of magnetic stone, which attracts iron, is a very minute world, which seems at variance with all other known matter. Nevertheless, how great have been the discoveries of which this little piece of metal has been instrumental! We owe the discovery of electricity entirely to this.

For my part, I do not consider this disdainful attitude as justifiable, and I believe that the facts of metapsychism, if they are true, ought to be loyally and methodically studied without hostility or favor—*sine ira ac studio.* We need not enquire whether the facts are in agreement [apparently] with facts already known, but whether they are genuine. Neither is it of importance to consider whether they concern a small or a great world, but whether they are true or false. This is the essential question; and the only way of forming an opinion on this question is to study it.

Now it is not possible, without absurd presumption, to decide on the truth or falsehood of a matter except after experiment. This is, in my humble opinion, one of the roads to be followed by the psychology of the future; for this route will be a fertile one. It will reveal to us unexpected horizons; vast regions, which were closed to us, will be opened.

I am quite aware of the strange character of these facts. But we must not allow ourselves to be scared by this strangeness. The duty of a savant lies precisely in this, that he should not let himself be dazzled by the science of the past, and that he should anticipate the science of the future. For if we consult the history of the sciences we shall see that every discovery, at its *debut,* has been treated, according to the times, as error or folly or crime.

And this was inevitable; because, characteristically, a discovery is always unforeseen, unexpected, novel; it runs counter to current opinion; it is not in accordance with classical, official teaching. If it were otherwise it would not be a discovery.

Also, as soon as it is announced, it is opposed by thousands of gainsayers. Even when it is very obvious, it is not accepted; and long discussions, supplemented by constantly repeated proofs, are necessary before it is admitted: because it is with difficulty that we bring ourselves to recognise the fact that we have hitherto lived in ignorance, and maintained errors.

We cannot conceive that there will come a day when all our science will appear childish and ridiculous. Our ancestors, the savants of the seventeenth century, were not fools, yet they had no notion of things, which now are regarded as elementary. A schoolboy of 15 years of age is, today, ten times more learned than Galileo, Newton and Lavoisier all put together. Are we to conclude, therefore, that Galileo, Newton and Lavoisier were fools? How could they possibly have known about photography, electrodynamism, the theory of microbes, and the telephone?

True, it is supposed that the progress of science will find its limit; and that there are no *essentially* new phenomena to be discovered. But this supposition seems to me puerile, and I prefer to think that the future is richer in discoveries to be made than the past in discoveries already made.

And in truth, if we look a little deeply into the questions, we shall see at once that our science— the science of which we are so proud—has not yet furnished us with an explanation of the things that it claims to know. The phenomena, which we observe, and of which we think we have discovered the laws, are not understood by us; and the laws are not laws but general *conditions*.

What surprises us and seems absurd is not the phenomenon, which we do not understand—for we do not understand anything about anything—but the phenomenon to which we are unaccustomed. A fact seems probably true because we have often witnessed it, and not at all because we have understood it; for none of the phenomena of nature are understood by us. We are not surprised to see a stone fall; for we are used to it. Nevertheless, although we can express in a formula the conditions of gravitation, we have not the slightest idea of its mechanism and its cause.

All facts—facts of psychology as well as the facts of the other sciences—may be classified in two groups: (1) Those which are habitual; (2) those which are rare and exceptional. The day will come when the exceptional facts will attract the interest of researchers as much as the ordinary facts. I could easily give you many curious accounts concerning metapsychical phenomena. But I must not take advantage of your patience. All the more because it is incumbent upon us to be very cautious in the *affirmation* of new truths.

The duty of science is (1) to be very daring—boundlessly audacious—in forming hypotheses; (2) to be very cautious—inexorably cautious—in affirmation.

I think I am acting in conformity with these equally important principles when, on the one hand, I recommend you not to neglect the study of metapsychical phenomena: because it seems to me that the future of psychology is linked with discovery in that realm; and, on the other hand, I urge those who devote their efforts to this study to cultivate prudence and patience.

Concluding Remarks

Richet continued to be puzzled about the nature of metapsychic phenomena until the end of his life. But he was hopeful. This is evident in his *Traité de Métapsychique* (1922) in which, like in the 1906 paper excerpted here, he continued to put his hope for metapsychics in future developments. In *Souvenirs d'un Physiologist*, Richet (1933b) referred to metapsychics as a discipline in an early stage of development, but stated: "I am convinced it is the science of the future" (p. 156). He felt that this science was the great hope of humanity (Richet, 1933a), and wrote in a book published the year he died that psychic phenomena, which he referred to as the inhabitual, "will have a place in science ... A new moral ideal will be the consequence, but not the basis of this new science" (Richet, 1935, p. 103).

Richet's essay represents a courageous attempt to defend psychical research in an important psychological forum, and a skeptical one at that. Unfortunately, like other defenders of psychical research, Richet's efforts were not successful in integrating the study of psychic phenomena with psychology. The two disciplines remain in an uneasy relationship to one another even today.

CHAPTER 5

The Traité de Métapsychique (1922)

~

As mentioned in Chapters 1 and 2, one of Richet's best-known works was his *Traité de Métapsychique* (1922b), which was later translated into English from its second edition (Richet, 1923b).[1] Richet had in mind the preparation of this book in 1905 when, in his Presidential Address to the Society for Psychical Research (SPR), he presented the term *métapsychique* (metapsychics) to refer to psychical research and mentioned that a possible title for his future book was *Traité de Métapsychique* (Richet, 1905, p. 13).

By the time the *Traité* was published in 1922, a topic discussed in previous chapters, Richet was well-known in psychical research. This was evident from the frequent and multiple citations he received in general French books about the topic (e.g., Coste, 1895, pp. v, xiii, 59, 101, 199, 221), as well as in other books published elsewhere (e.g., Podmore, 1897, pp. 84, 86, 223, 426).

The Content of the Traité

Richet states in the Preface that readers expecting "nebulous" discussions about "man's destiny, about magic, about theosophy" (Richet, 1922b, p. i) would be disappointed. Instead, he would write about facts without advancing a theory, because, in his view, theories in metapsychics were "astoundingly frail" (p. i).

The *Traité* is divided into four "books" or sections. The first is a general perspective on metapsychics, which was defined by Richet as "a science which object is phenomena, mechanical or psychological, due to seemingly intelligent forces or to unknown latent powers in human intelligence" (p. 5). In his view:

> Metapsychics—leaving aside, of course, psychology whose purpose is clearly limited—is the only science that studies intelligent forces. All the other forces that scholars have so far studied and analyzed, from the point of view of their causes and their effects, are blind forces, which do not have self-consciousness, devoid of caprice, in other words personality and willpower ... (p. 3).

This was not the case with metapsychic phenomena. Richet believed that they reflected will and intention in their operation.

Richet classified the field into subjective and objective metapsychics, terms he used to refer to mental and physical phenomena. The section also includes a discussion of history in which the author divided the subject into four periods. These periods were denominated by Richet as: mythical (up to Mesmer), magnetic (from Mesmer to the Fox sisters), spiritistic (from the Fox sisters to William Crookes), and scientific (starting with Crookes). Richet hoped that his book would start a fifth period.

Richet saw the scientific period as the high point of the history of interest in metapsychic phenomena and separated it conceptually and methodologically from previous movements. In fact, he pictured mesmerism, as well as Spiritism and Spiritualism, as stages in the development of metapsychics (on information about these topics see Appendix F.). Previous movements, Richet believed, had too much theory, something that metapsychics must be careful with. But he believed it would have been an injustice to despise the magnetizers and the spiritists. Their work, Richet stated, "contributed to the founding of metapsychics" (p. 40). But in his view their time was past. Nowadays a medium should not be wasted in informal spiritistic circles "without the use of methods of research adopted by all the sciences, balances, photography, cinematography, graphic registration. Similarly ... rigorous, strict investigation, similar to those the S.P.R. [Society for Psychical Research] has conducted, is indispensable" (p. 40). (See Appendix D. for an excerpt from the book's introduction regarding the scientific approach of metapsychics.)

The second part of the book is about "subjective metapsychics" (see Table 1). Richet started with a section in which he attempted to separate phenomena that could be explained via conventional ideas of the action of the subconscious mind such as automatisms, personation, and pantomnesia (or memories of all the past experiences of the person), from phenomena such as telepathy and the like requiring explanations beyond the conventional. This section is the topic of the next chapter.

Table 1
Summary of Topics of Richet's Discussion in the Second Part of the Traité About Subjective Metapsychics
Chapter 1: Subjective Metapsychics in General
Chapter 2: On Cryptesthesia (or Lucidity) in General   Chapter 3: Experimental Cryptesthesia
Chapter 4: The Divining Rod
Chapter 5: Animal Metapsychics
Chapter 6: Spontaneous Cryptesthesia

Two other sections were about chance and observation errors. Such discussions were not only proper in a book like this to show how psychical researchers have been aware of conventional explanations and the precautions they have taken to avoid them, but also served a rhetorical function in that they gave credibility to Richet's defenses of the reality of the metapsychic realm beyond the counter-explanations of science.

The rest of this part of the book is devoted to what Richet called *cryptesthesia*. This meant a "hidden sensibility, a perception of things, unknown regarding its mechanisms, and of which we cannot know but its effects" (p. 74). Richet discussed spontaneous and experimental examples of this faculty. He included his own observations and studies, such as those with a woman he referred to as Alice, and discussed the topic as manifested in mediums such as Leonora E. Piper (1857–1950), and in various ways, among them psychometry and premonitions. The spontaneous occurrences were classified as monitions involving non-serious and serious events (other than death), death, and those perceived collectively. Richet mentioned that cryptesthesia showed no time and space limitations. He wrote that the phenomenon "is very strange, and we do not understand it at all," but such lack of understanding did not mean the acceptance of spiritual entities following "savages who attributed forces of Nature to a Divinity" (p. 252).

Part 3 of the *Traité* is about physical phenomena (see Table 2). In addition to hauntings (and poltergeists), it includes chapters about telekinesis, materializations, levitation, and bilocation.

The latter was defined by Richet as the simultaneous presence of a person in different locations. He rejected the existence of objective bilocation as the duplication of the human body, but accepted that apparitions representing the individual could be perceived as if the person was alive and that this represented a modality of cryptesthesia.

Table 2
Summary of Topics of Richet's Discussion in the Third Part of the *Traité* About Objective Metapsychics
Chapter 1: On Objective Metapsychics in General
Chapter 2: Telekinesis
Chapter 3: Ectoplasms (Materializations)   Chapter 4: Levitations   Chapter 5: Bilocations   Chapter 6: Hauntings

Regardless of the fraudulent practices of some physical mediums, Richet was convinced that there were real telekinetic and ectoplasmic manifestations. Among many observations, he discussed medium Florence Cook and the famous Katie King materialization, and his own observations with medium Marthe Béraud. Regarding Béraud, Richet presented some notes he compiled in 1906 in which he saw ectoplasmic forms move and take shapes (see Appendix B.). He also mentioned in the book many other mediums, among them Linda Gazzera, D. D. Home, Eusapia Palladino, and Stanislawa Tomczyk.

In the conclusion, the fourth part of the book, Richet states that the collective weight of all evidence shows the reality of metapsychic phenomena. This, he believed, was the case regardless of criticisms:

Therefore: 1) there is in us a faculty of knowledge that is absolutely different from our common sensory faculties of knowledge (cryptesthesia); 2) movement of objects without contact are produced, even in plain light (telekinesis); 3) there are hands, bodies, objects, that appear to be formed completely from a cloud and show all the appearances of life (ectoplasmy); 4) there are presentiments that neither perspicacity nor chance can explain, and sometimes they are verified to their smallest details. (Richet, 1922b, p. 761.)

Also in the conclusion, Richet returned to his view that metapsychics should be an empirical specialty whose current task should not be the defense of particular models. In fact, if there was a perspective characterizing the *Traité* it was that of the need to have an ultra-empirical metapsychics with little theoretical content. Consistent with this view, Richet stated he was not convinced of any explanation so far offered to account for metapsychic phenomena and that at present (1922) no cohesive theory could be presented.

Richet was particularly critical of explanations based on the concept of discarnate action, something he discussed in other publications (e.g., Richet, 1924; see also Chapter 1). As he wrote in the *Traité*:

I do not condemn the spiritist theory. Surely it is premature: probably it is wrong. But it has had the immense merit of bringing about the experiences. It is one of those working hypotheses that Claude Bernard considered so fruitful. In any case, at least temporarily, as this theory is nothing unless proven, it is fragile, inconsistent, incoherent, we will content ourselves with saying ... that there are ways of transcendental knowledge that we cannot limit the scope of; that, consequently, we must attribute to this higher knowledge, of which the human brain sometimes seems endowed, all the powers which spiritists have attributed to spirits. (p. 781)

However, while he was not convinced, Richet admitted that for particular cases the simplest explanation seemed to be the discarnate agency one. This was the idea "that there are intelligent beings intervening in our life, and able to exercise some action over matter" (p. 757).

Nonetheless, and regardless of his protestations, Richet was not completely atheoretical. He was positive about the idea that unknown human faculties and forces were at work, and, as he discussed in the *Traité*, he used the concepts of personation and cryptesthesia to explain the manifestation of mental mediumship (see Chapter 6). Richet also speculated about forces in reference to materializations:

Materialization is a mechanical projection. ... Is it not a very long way to consider possible, other than projections of heat, light, and electricity, a projection of a mechanical force? The memorable demonstrations of Einstein establish to what extent mechanical energy is similar to luminous energy. (pp. 597–598)

Such an idea, while perhaps too vague to be called a theory, was consistent with an old model of biophysical forces present throughout the literatures of mesmerism, spiritualism, and psychical research.[2] However, Richet was cautions of several claims. He wrote:

The aura, the astral body, the perispirit, the odic effluvia, are various expressions to express the same phenomenon, a human (or animal) radiation. It is possible that this radiation exists, since everything is possible; but so far it has not been demonstrated. The day it is finally established, no doubt then we can relate it to everything that was said by Reichenbach, by A. de Rochas, by the old magnetisers,[3] and we would not be greatly surprised if this great discovery was made. It is unfortunately not yet, and there is not even a good beginning of proof. (p. 123)

Richet concluded his book with hope for the future, as he did in other publications. Currently, "when everything is still in darkness" (p. 793), Richet stated that there was a pressing need to move forward with research. "Then Metapsychics will come out of Occultism, as Chemistry was separated from Alchemy" (p. 793). The situation, Richet continued, may seem to be too dark and difficult to solve. He further wrote: "But this is no reason for not increasing our efforts and labors. ... The task is so beautiful that, even if we fail, the honor of having undertaken it gives some value to life" (p. 793).

Such views were consistent with Richet's general outlook on science. Like other scientists, he saw science as a slow process based on "patient, long, and difficult research" that could at best only promise to diminish slightly our overall ignorance (Richet, 1899, p. 35).

Facts and Theories

Richet's insistence on the collection of facts, to the neglect of theories, made the book his personal manifesto of psychical research. He projected an image of metapsychics as a science, arguing for the existence of a field that had a subject matter and a right to exist. But as much as the book was a summary of facts, it was also Richet's attempt to construct and promote the subject of metapsychics. However, in both the *Traité* and later publications, such as his autobiographical memoir published in *Souvenirs d'un Physiologiste* (Richet, 1933; translated and reprinted in Chapter 2), in which he described the discipline as being in a preliminary stage of development. Nonetheless, he stated in this later autobiographical essay that he considered metapsychics was the science of the future, something others had said before (e.g., Carrington, 1908).

Unfortunately, Richet's neglect to summarize theoretical models properly, and to include systematic discussions or research methodologies, weakens the status of the *Traité* as a rigorous textbook. I believe the empirical approach defended by Richet in the book would have received support in discussions of these topics.

Discussions of the Traité

This book received much publicity when it was first published in 1922. Richet presented it to the prestigious Académie des Sciences, referring to the phenomena in question as "new" and "inhabitual" (Richet, 1922a, p. 430). The reception of the *Traité* was surprising for an introductory book about psychical research. It was repeatedly reviewed as a special book. Examples of this are the long, and not always positive discussions of it, in journals dedicated to psychic phenomena such as *Luce e Ombra* (Bozzano, 1922), *Psychische Studien* (Driesch, 1924), the *Journal of the American Society for Psychical Research* (Holt, 1922), the *Proceedings of the Society for Psychical Research* (Lodge, 1923), and the *Revue Métapsychique* (Sudre, 1922).[4]

For example, English physicist and psychical researcher Oliver J. Lodge (1851–1940) stated that, in discussing the evidence for survival of death, Richet's hope and endeavour are "to trace and attribute everything to the normal faculties of man, without bringing in outside and hypothetical influences of any kind whatsoever. Not that he is foolishly dogmatic enough to deny the possibility of such influences, but because he considers that they are beyond the scope of present science; and his object is to be purely scientific" (Lodge, 1923, p. 83).

But in doing so, Lodge believed, Richet tended to minimize evidence for survival and to overemphasize critical facts.

Other examples were comments appearing in French sources. A writer in the literary magazine *Mercure de France* referred to the *Traité* as the event of the day (Olivier, 1922), and an entry about the book appeared in *Larousse Mensuel Illustré* (Challaye, 1920–1922). Two newspapers had front page discussions of the book, *L'Ouest-Éclair* (Bricout, 1923), and *Le Figaro* (de Fleury, 1922), and various notices of the book also were published in *La Croix* (Latour, 1922), *L'Illustration* (Bourget, 1922), *Le Journal* (Chassaigne, 1922), and *Le Petit Parisien* (Anonymous, 1922c), among other newspapers.

The *Traité* was also commented on in scholarly publications. This included various medical journals, among them the *Revue de Pathologie Comparée et de l'Hygiene* (Blier, 1922), *Presse Médicale* (Hartenberg, 1924), *L'Encéphale* (Levy-Valensi, 1922), and the *Journal de l'Association Médicale Mutualle* (N., 1922).[5]

Considering the long history of negative critiques and rejection of psychic claims (e.g., Hall, 1887; Jastrow, 1889), it is not surprising that there were several negative evaluations of the *Traité*.[6] Two prominent examples of negative reviews appearing in the journals of other disciplines were those authored by psychopathologist Pierre Janet (1859–1947) and psychologist Henri Piéron (1881–1964), who cast doubt on the reality of psychic phenomena and on the validity of metapsychics as a scientific discipline (Janet, 1923; Piéron, 1922). Janet argued that "in the presence of facts that strongly work up our suspicions, our doubts … he [Richet] does not seem to be moved and keeps the same unalterable faith" (p. 30). Janet was surprised that Richet could be so sure that in some specific instances no fraud took place, and more, that no fraud was possible with mediums (which was not Richet's position). Such complete belief was not only inadmissible to Janet, but he felt that this attitude undermined readers' confidence in Richet's critical sense.

There is no question that the book was comprehensive and systematic, and this made it valuable as a general introduction to the subject. Regardless of its faults, it is, in fact, one of the best overviews of psychical research for the period in question.

Why Did the Book Receive So Much Attention?

For many, particularly in France, the *Traité* became an exemplar of the "new" science, and this took place in spite of much criticism. Why, one may ask, did Richet's book attain such a status? After all, the content of *Traité* was not innovative or revolutionary, so why did it command so much attention and respect? In fact, in many ways the *Traité* was rather dry and uninspired. I believe there are at least three reasons for its prominence.

First, Richet's book cannot be dismissed as just a relatively unimportant exercise in synthesis. In fact, this characteristic of the book is one of the aspects identified by Ceccarelli (2001) as being important to produce influential books that assist in the development of interdisciplinary communities. Synthesis is present in the *Traité* in the form of a modest non-theoretical integration based on the accumulation of facts presented to show the existence of a phenomenon.[7]

Ceccarelli believes that such influential books present two other characteristics: the development of an "authorial persona," and the fact that the text is addressed to more than one audience. The first point, perhaps, includes Richet's strong and repeated ultra-empirical statements about facts and anti-survival stances,[8] while the second may also be present in that several audiences benefited from the work: scientists, psychical researchers, and the general public. While I do not want to push this view too much, it seems to me that the book could be studied in more detail from this perspective.

Second, and as briefly discussed in Chapter 1, the author commanded much attention due to his eminence.

Richet—who worked in such various fields as aviation, eugenics, history, literature, pacifism, philosophy, psychical research, psychology, and sociology—was a well-known and highly respected intellectual. He published much research on physiological topics such as animal heat, breathing, stomach acid, serotherapy, and anaphylaxis (Wolf, 1993). As early as 1879, he was referred to in an American medical journal as being "well-known to the medical public as one of the rising younger Frenchmen of scientific tastes and ability, already the author of several works of merit" (Putnam, 1879, p. 815).

He also had several important academic positions and honors before the publication of *Traité*. These included being editor of the *Revue Scientifique*, Professor of Physiology at the Faculté de Médicine in Paris, member of the Académie de Médicine and of the Académie des Sciences, and Nobel Prize winner for his work on anaphylaxis. In addition, Richet had many social advantages. His wealth and high social position, coming both from his father and from his mother's family, allowed him many personal connections that facilitated publishing and being heard in different forums (on these issues, see Wolf, 1993). All this gave Richet a special status, a persona that many others perceived as a man worth listening to.

All this meant that a treatise about psychic phenomena from such a man would not be ignored and would be seen as a more important event than publications on the topic by less eminent individuals. His persona was a social and intellectual beacon that attracted many, who would either praise or condemn him for his positive belief in the existence of metapsychic phenomena and for his involvement with the topic.

Finally, and interacting with what I have said above, was the fact that, as seen in some studies about French psychical research (e.g., Brower, 2010; Evrard, 2016), the 1920s were busy years in France for metapsychics, making the *Traité* of great interest to those open to the subject, and a cause of embarrassment and worry for skeptics. The period presented many public controversies, several of which were related to physical mediumship. This consisted of:

> Feats of mediums, the testimony of metapsychists, the severe reproaches of some skeptical authors ... A whole literature developed and polarized the debate between, on the one hand, the advocates of the existence of physical phenomena, and, on the other, the adversaries who denied the authenticity of the phenomena (Gutierez & Maillard, 2005, pp. 184–185)

The Institut Métapsychique International was founded in 1919, and its journal appeared in 1920, bringing together, in their Board of Directors, individuals such as Richet, French engineer and spiritist leader Gabriel Delanne (1857–1926), French astronomer Camille Flammarion (1842–1925), French physician Gustave Geley (1868–1924), and Italian physician Rocco Santoliquido (1854–1930). Its Director, Geley (1919), wrote in the newspaper *Le Journal* that he had great hopes that this organization would help metapsychics to organize and develop. Many of these developments were chronicled in the Institute's journal; among them were séances with Polish materialization medium Franek Kluski (Geley, 1921).

The general public was exposed to many newspaper discussions of the topic. This included articles about a public competition sponsored by *Le Matin* in which applicants had to produce particular forms of psychic phenomena to win a cash prize depending on a committee's deliberations (Anonymous, 1922a). Similarly, the journalist and critic of psychical research Paul Heuzé (1878-1938) published in the newspaper *L'Opinion* several articles interviewing scientists and intellectuals involved with psychic phenomena, such as Richet, the Belgian writer Maurice Maeterlinck (1862–1949), and the famous Polish scientist Marie Curie (1867–1934) (Heuzé, 1921a). Later articles were negative views of various physical mediums: among them was Eva C. (Heuzé, 1922a).[9]

Partly because of Heuzé, medium Eva C., known before as Marthe Béraud, was investigated by a committee of scientists at the Sorbonne, which concluded that the medium had not presented evidence for the phenomenon of materialization (Lapicque, Dumas, Piéron, & Laugier, 1922). This was discussed in even more negative ways in the press, as seen in an article by Heuzé (1922b). But there were also examples during the 1920s of positive discussions about psychic phenomena in France.[10]

The Traité Today

The *Traité* is still discussed today as an important work from a previous era (e.g., Alvarado, 2016; Brower, 2010, pp. 124–125). Modern researchers will find it of value for several reasons.

The book is a reference work presenting many summaries of studies, bibliographical sources, and evidential claims about psychic phenomena for the pre-1922 period. In addition, those current researchers who are not familiar with the old psychical research literature will find, in this book, a window into the past; a past somewhat different from the present, as seen in the emphasis on gifted subjects, such as psychics and mediums, on the phenomena of physical mediumship, and on the issue of survival of death.

CHAPTER 6

Richet on "The Limits of Psychic and Metapsychic Science"

~

I n Chapters 1 and 5 I mentioned some of Richet's ideas to explain mediumship in non-psychic ways, via unconscious processes. In this chapter I focus on this topic via a presentation of a long excerpt from one of Richet's writings, the above-mentioned *Traité*.

Conventional Explanations of Mediumship

Some of this conceptual tradition of conventional explanations includes the ideas of individuals who have discussed mediumship and other phenomena, assuming that automatisms and psychopathology could account for the observations reported. Examples from the late nineteenth-century are writings such as William Carpenter's (1813-1885) *Mesmerism and Spiritualism, &c. Historically and Scientifically Considered* (1877), as well as the work of others (e.g., Hammond, 1876; Janet, 1889).[1] Furthermore, there were several discussions of the concept of iatrogenic creation of mediumistic communication, as seen in critiques of the reincarnation content of some communications (Aksakof, 1875). Both Théodore Flournoy (1854–1920) and Joseph Maxwell (1858–1938) discussed the creation of mediumistic personalities as a function of suggestion (Flournoy, 1900; Maxwell, 1903/1905).[2] As stated by one of them:

> We must ... take into consideration the enormous suggestibility and auto-suggestibility of mediums, which render them so sensitive to all the influences of spiritistic reunions, and are so favorable to the play of those brilliant subliminal creations in which, occasionally, the doctrinal ideas of the surrounding environment are reflected together with the latent emotional tendencies of the medium herself (Flournoy, 1900, p. 443).

Others, such as Frederic W.H. Myers, offered conventional explanations of mediumistic phenomena that involved subconscious creativity, but also included psychic phenomena such as telepathy between the living (Myers, 1884). In fact Myers (1903) argued that the majority of supernormal phenomena "are due to the action of the still embodied spirit of the agent or percipient himself" (Vol. 1, p. 6). Later researchers defending human agency through phenomena such as telepathy included Flournoy (1911). There was also a group of writers who argued that physical mediumship could be explained through human agency (e.g., Rogers, 1853; Sudre, 1926).[3]

Richet on the Abilities of the Unconscious Mind

I am presenting here an excerpt about this topic taken from the English translation of Richet's *Traité* (Richet, 1923). At the beginning of the book Richet discussed conventional explanations of some psychic phenomena. These included the creative and memory capabilities of the unconscious mind. Furthermore, Richet followed previous writers and discussed the idea that the capabilities of the unconscious mind could include the acquisition of supernormal information.

Richet's emphasis on the capabilities of the unconcious is not surprising considering his previous writings on the "objectification of types," or the creation of personalities under hypnosis with amnesia of the person's own identity (Richet, 1883). Referring to mediumship, Richet (1884) stated "all the intelligent manifestations attributed to the spirits are due to an individual that is unconscious and active at the same time" (p. 650). Some years later, in his Presidential Address to the Society for Psychical Research, Richet (1905) referred to the phenomena of hypnotic personifications where it was evident that no spirit influence was present. He wondered if the personifications that "play a large role in spiritism were but phenomena of the same genre" (p. 45).

The following is a long excerpt in which Richet discusses these ideas.

The Limits of Psychic and Metapsychic Science

A primary difficulty confronts us, for as soon as we can explain any phenomenon of lucidity by extreme acuteness of intelligence or by systematic treatment of the subconscious, it is clear that there is no need to refer it to metapsychics, i.e., to assume unknown faculties or the intervention of external intelligences. It will suffice to say that it is only the effect of exceptional human acuteness. We are, therefore, bound first to investigate the limits to human intelligence.

This is exceedingly difficult, for many intellectual phenomena occur quite apart from consciousness; and these have belonged to normal psychology since the time of Leibnitz. The mind can work without the assistance of consciousness; very complex intellectual processes take place unknown to us, and a whole world of ideas vibrates in us of which we are unconscious. Probably no remembrance of the past is completely effaced; consciously we forget much, but memory forgets nothing; the mass of past impressions is retained almost intact, though consciousness of them has vanished. For the subconsciousness wakes and works side by side with sleeping consciousness, and there can be no doubt that comparisons, associations, and judgments are formed in which the conscious self takes no part. The importance of these phenomena of the subconscious cannot be over-emphasized; but as everything that can be explained by normal psychology should be eliminated from metapsychics, and as the subconscious work of the mind pertains to normal psychology, we must lay down and always remember the law—subconsciousness is competent to do everything that consciousness can do.

Our senses give us our notions of things, and we know those things by what our senses bring us ... but rearrangements of sensorial data may make our notions extremely complex. Thus the subconscience can construct poetry, discourses, drama, and mathematics everything that consciousness can construct. Nevertheless all this wealth is reconstructive; intelligence, whether conscious or subconscious, can never furnish more than it has been given unless we suppose some new faculty of cognition to exist. Intelligence can only work on material supplied by normal sensorial channels.

To quote a well-known simile, a mill is excellent for grinding, but can never produce anything but what it has been given to grind.

Let us suppose that Helen Smith[4] has never heard a word of Sanscrit nor read or seen any Sanscrit book. Then if she should speak or write in Sanscrit—i.e., re-invent that language—I should consider the event miraculous, and a metapsychic phenomenon; for no human intelligence could do this.

Before drawing so extreme an inference, however, my reluctance to admit the supernormal will oblige me to make all possible suppositions. It must first be established that she has never opened a Sanscrit book, and such proof is not easy to get; for even if her good faith is assured she may have forgotten that one day in some public or private library she turned over the leaves of such a book. Besides, the Sanscrit phrase must not be a mere quotation, but have reference to present circumstances. The conditions necessary to scientific conviction of the transcendental nature of the phenomenon are so onerous that I doubt if they can often be found concurrent.

Similarly A., an unpoetical person who has never written any verse, composes poems showing delicate and original poetic faculty while in a mediumistic state. She thus writes several volumes of verse, dictating so rapidly as to make it difficult to follow. This is certainly very surprising; but before supposing that some external intelligence intervenes I shall make the simpler hypothesis that she has subconscious poetic faculty. Her verses, however good, do not transcend human intelligence.

I know that spiritualists and occultists will exclaim against this as they did against my learned friend, T. Flournoy.[5] But their objections are not justified, for it lies on them to prove the intervention of extraneous intelligence; and this proof can be given only by establishing the absolute incapacity of subconscious intelligence to write the verse or to remember certain scraps of Sanscrit.

Laplace says somewhere, the rigour of proof must be proportionate to the gravity of the conclusion. Now to admit that an extra-terrene intelligence moves the brain of Helen Smith to inspire her with Sanscrit, or the brain of A. to dictate French verse, is an inference so contrary to common-sense and logic that I shall admit any hypothesis short of mathematical or physical impossibility, rather than that of an extra-terrene mind. It is reasonable to suppose that Helen Smith has retained in an impeccable memory some phrases of Sanscrit read ten years before, and that A. may subconsciously construct verses as rapidly as a professional poet.

Every normal hypothesis must be exhausted, and also the subconscious work of the mind and the resources of an infallible memory, before we can dare to affirm the intervention of another intelligence ...

On my asking Stella[6] for the name of one of the women who tended my infancy, she replied, "Melanie." I was not thinking of Melanie, and I am most positively sure that this name, which disappeared out of my life fifty years ago, and which I have not thought of for those fifty years, has never been uttered by me. In this case I am obliged to infer a metapsychic phenomenon, for neither pantomnesia nor subconscious mentation working up old remembrances can account for this name emerging. I put chance on one side.

It will then be no matter for astonishment if we refuse to admit, as metapsychic, various phenomena that present a metapsychic aspect to credulous persons. By the joint action of pantomnesia[7] and the subconscious working of the mind, some persons can produce poetical, fanciful, or scientific work of a complex and very wonderful nature, but which ought not to surprise us more than if they were consciously produced.

Stella in her normal state never composes poetry, but in her mediumistic state dictates, through the table, verses, sometimes of high merit, on a subject given to her and in a prescribed number of words. But I may say, without vanity, that I myself, simultaneously, by a kind of collaboration with Petrarch, who (according to the table) was speaking through Stella, was able to compose four lines on a given subject in a required number of words; and this poetry to order was neither better nor worse than that of "Petrarch." I prefer to suppose that Stella composed unconsciously what I was able to compose consciously; at any rate, that is much simpler than to suppose the intervention of Petrarch.

In a mediumistic state, Victorien Sardou drew a curious and well-known design entitled The House of Mozart.[8] Nothing could be more strange, but I shall always feel it simpler to admit that the genius of Sardou did the subconscious work than to imagine that the soul of Mozart moved Sardou's muscles.

Every case must carefully be scrutinized before it is admitted as genuinely metapsychic; but the delicate and difficult process of analyzing such cases will lead us … to the conclusion that there is a small number of subjective intellectual facts (much less numerous than spiritualists suppose), which neither pantomnesia nor the subconscious elaboration of remembrances can account for.

Nevertheless, even the facts inexplicable by pantomnesia do not necessarily imply the presence of an external intelligence; for yet another hypothesis is possible-that human intelligence has a greater range than that we are accustomed to attribute to it ...

There may be other senses than the five known to us. Some animals, pigeons for instance, have a sense of direction that escapes our analysis. Why should there be no cognitive faculties other than our senses? We think that the magnet, though it acts upon iron, does not act on our nervous centres; but if it were discovered that it does, I for one should not be greatly surprised. Wireless telegraphy has shown us that messages can be transmitted through space; it is therefore possible that by an analogous but invisible mechanism to which our instruments and our senses are insensitive, the brain may be affected without our being able to perceive anything either of the transmitter or the receiver. It is our ignorance that confines all possible knowledge of the external world to our five senses.

Accordingly, before inferring the existence of extraneous intelligence, I willingly admit, as a provisional hypothesis, that there are in us cognitive faculties as yet undetermined, neither usual nor of daily occurrence, but irregular in their appearance and mysterious in their action.[9]

That is metapsychics, and we have to decide between two hypotheses.

1. Does an external intelligence act on ours?

2. Is our intelligence endowed with a new faculty of cognition?

Subjective phenomena alone are not sufficient for a decision between these two hypotheses; it will be necessary to examine ... whether the aggregate evidence pointing to extra-terrene intelligence is sufficient to prove either the hypothesis that human intelligence is endowed with faculties new to us; or, that extraneous *intelligences incorporate and incarnate themselves in humanity* ...

We learn from psychology that pantomnesia exists, and also that the subconscious, perhaps even more than the conscious, is capable of prolonged and skilful elaboration of its materials.

In fine, [*sic*] in order to distinguish between the psychological and the metapsychic we shall adopt the criterion: *Everything that the human intelligence can do, even when it is most profound and penetrating, is psychological. Everything of which such intelligence is incapable belongs to metapsychics.*

If Helen Smith, without having read or heard a single word of Sanscrit, speaks it fluently and correctly, that would be metapsychic, for no human intelligence can reconstruct a language. A., thinking herself inspired by her "guide," composes verses quickly and well; this is psychological, for many persons, and perhaps A., among them, can do the same.

Stella tells me the name of an old servant of my parents fifty years ago. This is metapsychic, for she has certainly never heard me pronounce that name; and no intelligence, conscious or unconscious, could give that name without having heard it.

T. leaves his friend J. in good health. He see his friend's apparition, notes the hour, and says, "J. died at nine o'clock in the evening." This is metapsychic, for no normal psychological process could have revealed it. Thus the work of analysis, demanding most scrupulous care, will be to examine whether the facts under consideration are explicable by known mental laws, or whether it is not necessary ... to suppose the existence of a special sensitiveness which I call cryptesthesia—a new faculty of cognition, called lucidity by ancient authors and telepathy by modern ones (Richet, 1923, pp. 45–55).

Concluding Remarks

Richet's thoughts are representative of different aspects of the conceptual history of psychical research. For example, they show the constant struggle between survival and non-survival explanations of psychic phenomena when human faculties are postulated to account for manifestations such as mediumistic communications. Earlier discussions such as those of Flournoy (1900) and Myers (1884, 1903), among others, inspired Richet's arguments.

At the same time, the excerpt from Richet illustrates that area of phenomena that Hyslop (1906) referred to as the "borderland of psychical research." These were phenomena that allowed us to distinguish the normal and the abnormal from the supernormal, and as such had an important and practical use for the psychical researcher. Such area included phenomena such as hallucinations, illusions and psychophysiological manifestations, and the capabilities of the unconscious mentioned by Richet in the excerpt: creativity, detailed memory, and changes of personality. The latter has been very important in the histories of both hypnosis and secondary personalities, areas to which Richet (1883), and others were important contributors during the nineteenth century and later.[10]

While some of the above mentioned figures—particularly Myers and Flournoy—made more valuable and detailed contributions to the topic in question than Richet did, the latter contributed much to publicize the idea that: "The talents of the unconscious show even more variety that those of consciousness" (Richet, 1923, p. 44).

Appendix A

Richet on Leonora Piper

~

I present here a rarely cited short report written in French by Charles Richet, which I have translated into English.

Richet wrote repeatedly about Mrs. Piper throughout his career (e.g., Richet, 1905, pp. 45–46; 1922, pp. 165–175). The account of his experiences with Piper presented here appeared as part of Walter Leaf's (1890) paper about the medium reporting séances held in 1889 in England. In the report it was pointed out that Richet was present in two seances on 6 and 8 December (Leaf, 1890, pp. 629, 630). Leaf's report was part of the well-known series of papers entitled "A Record of Observations of Certain Phenomena of Trance" which appeared in the *Proceedings of the Society for Psychical Research* in 1890 and dealt with the investigation of Piper in 1889 by several members of the Society for Psychical Research. These papers included an introduction by Frederic W.H. Myers (1890), long reports of seances by Oliver Lodge (1890a) and Walter Leaf (1890), and an account by William James (1890) of his initial contact with Mrs. Piper in the United States in the form of a letter that he sent to Myers. The issue of the *Proceedings* also included an index of séance incidents prepared by Lodge (1890b). Appearing after James' (1886) initial report about the medium, the papers by Lodge and Leaf were the first major systematic and evidential published reports about Piper, which were followed some years later by the work of Richard Hodgson (1892, 1898; who started his research before the 1889 sittings in England) and others (e.g., Hyslop, 1901; Newbold, 1898).

The short account by Richet, presented below, has probably been neglected because it was written in French and because it does not contribute much evidential material nor anything new that has not been reported in more detail elsewhere. Furthermore, the report is easy to overlook because it is embedded within Leaf's (1890) article (see pp. 618–620).

Here is a translation of Richet's remarks.

Madam P. shows, so to speak, the transition between the clairvoyant spiritist mediums, as they are known in America, and the somnambulists that we know in France.

We do not put her to sleep by the procedure of magnetic passes, but she enters *trance*, so to speak, spontaneously.

However all does not happen spontaneously, for she needs to grab someone's hand for the **trance**. Then she takes the hand, for a few minutes remaining in silence and in half-darkness. After some time—from 5 to 15 minutes—she has small spasmodic convulsions that increase, ending with a very moderate small epileptiform seizure. At the end of this crisis she falls into a state of stupor, with a somewhat gasping breathing, which lasts close to a minute or two; then, all of a sudden, she comes out of this stupor by an outburst. Her voice has changed; it is no longer Mrs. P. who is there, but another character, Dr. Phinuit, who speaks with a deep voice, of manly appearance, with a mixed black patois, and a French and American dialect accent.

It is a question whether Dr. Phinuit really presents phenomena of lucidity, and if the names he gives of different characters seen or heard around the observer are actually real.

It is noteworthy that in most experiments the observer does not part with Mrs. P.'s hand.

Here is the result of my observations, from the point of view of lucidity.

The first name she gave me is the name *Marie Anne*; but she did not give it in response to a question from me. It turns out that the name Marie Anne was involved in an episode of my youth which would be too long to tell here, and which was, in any case, absolutely unknown to all persons at Cambridge.

I asked some details about Marie Anne; she told me errors, except this fact, which is true, that she lived near the schoolhouse.

It seems that Mrs. P. did not know my name: but I admit as very possible that she knew it, or that people of the house had spoken it inadvertently, or that she guessed my nationality. (She was around Mr. William James and Mr. Hodgson for two years, and had read the *Proceedings* of the American Society for Psychical Research.) She told me that my name was *Charles*, and that I worked in medicine. Then I told her about my grandfather: she told me his name was *Charles* like me, which is true, although I had told her it was my mother's father. She added that he was called *Richhet*, and she said each letter unaided by me and spontaneously. But I cannot attach much importance to these facts because it is quite possible that she knew my name unconsciously.

Then I asked a few details about my grandfather. She had nothing to say, but very inaccurate and numerous mistakes; assuring me he was a soldier—a chemist—a doctor—that I lived with him—that he had a dog; all incorrect facts. I told him he had translated an American author into French. It was impossible to say whom. She said, Henry James, Hawthorne, &c., without being able to say Franklin.

Because she talked about a dog, I asked her about a little dog I had that was dead. She said *Pick* without hesitation. Now this fact is very important, and it is, in my opinion, the best result she gave; because my dog was called *Dick*; and we must admit she absolutely did not know the name, which was unknown at Cambridge and at Boston.

Other questions about the number of children were followed by complete failure. She said successively, 4–3–2–5–1, without been able to say the exact number, nor their names.

The next day, I *thought* to ask her the name of a person in my family long dead, whose name was given to me in the first experiments in spiritism that I made. I spoke to Mr. Myers in the course of the day without telling him the name of this person, absolutely unknown to him and everyone. In addition, I thought, mentally, that it would be interesting to ask again some details about my grandfather, in particular my grandmother's nickname; but I said nothing to anyone.

However, in the course of the experiment on Monday, giving her hand to Miss X, she said the name *Louise*, who did not apply at all to Miss X., which is precisely the name I was looking for. In addition she said the name *Renoi*, which did not apply to Miss. X at all, but which had the first letters of the name of my grandfather, a name she did not know. (This name was however printed in the *Proceedings of the Society for Psychical Research*.) It is true that neither the name Louise nor the name Renoi have been attributed to me or to some persons from my family by Mrs. Piper; which greatly diminishes the value of their meaning, since what Mrs. Piper said was not addressed to me, but to Miss. X.

Addressing me, Mrs. Piper said, "I'll tell you about *Adéla*." Adéla is the name of my grandmother. It is true that Mrs. Piper could not tell me what my family connections were with Adéla.

For completeness, I must mention a curious fact. She said, "You have pills in your pocket," and touching them with her finger, she felt them, and peeled them—and without tasting them, she boldly and without hesitation said, "This is quinine"; which was right. The experience would have been much more interesting if it had been about something else less common than quinine ...

In short, to sum up these facts, there is in my experiences with Mrs. Piper but one indisputable fact of lucidity: because I do not attach any value to replies made to a question. This is the name of *Pick* for *Dick*: which certainly nothing could have given an indication of. It is chance or lucidity; it cannot be anything else.

As for [Mrs. Piper's] good faith (conscious), this is absolutely certain; and for every observer used to seeing somnambules, the state of Madam Piper certainly is the same as the state of somnambules in magnetic sleep, with changes in personality. [in Leaf, 1890, pp. 618-620]

Appendix B

Observations of Moving Ectoplasm by Richet

~

Here are some excerpts of Richet's observations with medium Marthe Béraud taken from *Thirty Years of Psychical Research* (New York: Macmillan, 1923).

In the quite small room, which I search thoroughly, a corner, curtains that can be closed and opened before the corner; a cane chair in the middle on which Marthe sits. Mme. de S., whom I will call A., is alone with Marthe and myself. We both sit close to Marthe ... The light is an electric lamp covered with red material, and gives light enough to show all the white in Marthe's garments and the white ribbons in her hair. After about half an hour, I open the curtains and see a faint luminosity on the floor, so feeble that I doubt its reality. By degrees this light increases; it is like a small, luminous handkerchief lying on the floor ... The luminous spot grows; its outlines are milky, undefined and cloudy ... It approaches the chair, increases in size, and takes a serpentine form which tends to rise towards the left arm of A.'s chair. Its outlines become sharper; it is like a mass of half-empty fabric. Then follows an extraordinary sight: a point detaches itself from the mass, mounts up, bends and directs itself to Marthe's breast, her hands being held the whole time. The point continues to advance in a terrifying way like an animal pointing its beak; and, as it advances, on the rigid stalk there appears a thin gauzy structure like a bat's wing, so thin and transparent that Marthe's garments can be seen through it ...

I can approach and look very closely, only an inch away. I see what looks like a swollen substance, moving as if alive, and changing its form. For five or six minutes I examine it attentively. I see extensions like the horns of a snail, which start up to right and left; these horns are like transparent gelatin, they project from and sink back into the more defined central mass. (p. 516)

Appendix C
On the Term Ectoplasm
~

The actual first appearance of the term ectoplasm is uncertain, even though Richet has been credited with it repeatedly and Richet (1922, p. 656) himself claimed that he invented it in relationship to his observations with Palladino (see Granger, 2014). He wrote about early seances, which he had with this medium (see Lodge, 1894; Richet, 1895): "In seances with Lodge, Myers, Ochorowicz, every time we were touched, we said, half jokingly, 'an ectoplasm again!' " (Richet, 1922, p. 637, footnote).

Historian Andreas Sommer informs me that he found a letter in the Aksakof papers at Pushkinskij Dom, St. Petersburg, suggesting that this was Ochorowicz's term. In the letter Myers wrote to Aksakof on August 3, 1894 stating, "we rather tend to use sometimes Ochorowicz's word—Ectoplasm." Furthermore, and as pointed out by Demarest (2013), the term had been in use previously in biological literature with a different meaning, suggesting that Richet must have taken it from that context.

Interestingly, and unrelated to the origin of the term, Richet (1922) was using it in later years to refer to the "forms coming out of the body of Eusapia" (p. 637) and to "kind of a gelatinous protoplasm, amorphous at first" (p. 656), which leaves the body of the medium, and which takes shapes later. Ectoplasms, he went on to say in relation to medium Marthe Béraud, showed movement: it "crawls like an animal, rises from the ground, grows tentacles like an amoeba. It is not attached to the body of the medium during the whole time, but more often it emanates from, and is connected to it" (p. 665).

Appendix D
Is There a Science of Metapsychics?

This is taken from Richet's
Thirty Years of Psychical Research
(New York: Macmillan, 1923)

~

Is There a Science of Metapsychics?

This question must be put, for, to many men of science, none of the alleged facts in the domain of "magnetism" or spiritualism deserve serious consideration. They say, "A science cannot be constructed out of gossip; and the accounts you bring us are nothing more. The hallucinations with all their wealth of detail described by simple people are matter for the alienist, and the performances of mediums are vulgar frauds. Mediums who claim supernatural powers and allege that they are intermediaries between the dead and the living, are either hallucinated or tricksters. As soon as precautions are taken against credulity and fraud, the error or the imposture is always manifest. No undeniable fact of lucidity or movement of objects without contact has ever been established before a committee of enquiry composed of men of scientific standing. If chance, mal-observation, and trickery are eliminated, nothing remains of the so-called metapsychics but a vast illusion. The stricter the conditions, the slighter the phenomena become, till they vanish altogether. A science that claims to be experimental but relies on experiments that cannot be reproduced is no science at all. You affirm extraordinary and unbelievable things that upset all that science has hitherto accepted as true, but you cannot prove them, for up to the present such proof has evaded all methodical research. It is not for us to prove that the facts you affirm are false; it is for you to prove that they are true."

"Further, even if we were to see these strange facts, we should think ourselves tricked or hallucinated, for your work lies among impostors, and the things you affirm are too absurd to be true."

Such is the kind of language used by honourable men of science who deny the reality of all metapsychic phenomena. If they were right, this book would be absolutely useless, even ridiculous; and might be entitled "A Treatise on an Error." But, these facts exist, and are called occult only because they are not understood.

We have read and re-read, studied and analyzed the works written on these subjects, and we declare it vastly improbable, and even impossible, that eminent and upright men such as Sir William Crookes, Sir Oliver Lodge, Reichenbach, A. Russel Wallace, Lombroso, William James, Schiaparelli, F. W. H. Myers, Zöllner, A. de Rochas, Ochorowicz, Morselli, Sir William Barrett, Ed. Gurney, C. Flammarion, and many others, in spite of their close attention and their scientific knowledge, should all have been duped over and over again a hundred times by tricksters or have been the victims of an astounding credulity. It is not possible that they should all, and always, have been so blind as not to perceive frauds necessarily gross; so incautious as to form conclusions where no conclusion was legitimately possible; and so unskillful as never to have made a single unexceptionable experiment. A priori, their experiments deserve careful consideration and not to be contemptuously rejected.

The history of all sciences warns us that the simplest discoveries have been rejected a priori, as being incompatible with science. Medical anesthesia was denied by Majendie. The action of microbes was contested for twenty years by all the scientists of all the academies. Galileo was imprisoned for saying that the earth revolves. Bouillaud declared that the telephone was but ventriloquism. Lavoisier said that stones cannot fall from the sky, for there are no stones in the sky. The circulation of the blood was only admitted after forty years of sterile discussion. In a lecture in 1827 at the Academy of Sciences, my great-grandfather, P. S. Girard, considered it folly to suppose that water could be led to the upper floors of houses by pipes. In 1840, J. Müller declared that the speed of nerve impulses could never be measured. In 1699, Papin constructed the first steamboat; a hundred years later Fulton rediscovered the possibility of steam navigation, but it was not applied till twenty years later. When in 1892, under the guidance of my distinguished master, Marey, I made my first attempt in aviation, I met with only incredulity, contempt, and sarcasm. A volume might be written on the absurd criticisms with which every great discovery has been received.

This is not a matter of the opinions of the crowd, which are of no importance; they are the opinions of scientists, who imagine that they have laid down boundaries that science cannot overpass. These boundaries soon become milestones on the road of progress, as Flammarion remarks. When such men declare that such and such a phenomenon is impossible, they make an unfortunate confusion between what is contradictory of known laws and what is new. This must be emphasized, for it is the cause of disastrous misunderstandings . . .

Every new truth necessarily appears highly improbable; such, however, are of frequent occurrence in the evolution of the sciences, and as soon as a discoverer enunciates one it excites opposition. Instead of testing, men deny it . . .

Everything of which we are ignorant appears improbable, but the improbabilities of today are the elementary truths of tomorrow.

Among the discoveries which by reason of my advanced age I have seen developed under my own eyes, so to speak, I will take four which in 1875 would have seemed absurdly inadmissible:

1. The voice of an individual speaking in Paris can be heard in Rome. (Telephone.)
2. The germs of all diseases can be bottled and cultivated in a cupboard. (Bacteriology.)
3. The bones of a living person can be photographed. (X-rays.)
4. Five hundred guns can be taken through the air at a speed of 180 miles an hour. (Aëroplanes.)

Anyone who uttered such audacities in 1875 would have been thought a dangerous lunatic.

Our routine-keeping intelligence is such that it rejects anything to which it is unaccustomed, and from a careful study of the facts around us, we should be content to say, there are some that are usual and some that are unusual. We ought to say no more than this and, above all we should be careful not to make two classes—facts that are understood, and facts that are not understood. For in truth we really understand nothing, absolutely nothing, of the truths of science, whether great or small . . .

What is matter? Is it continuous or discontinuous? What is electricity? Is the hypothesis of the ether really understood by those who accept it? We see a stone fall back when thrown upwards; do we, therefore, understand gravitation? Two gases combine to form a new body in which the same atoms as in the gases are found; have we really understood what has taken place? Why should such and such an ovule, fertilized by a certain zoosperm, produce an oak-tree, a bear-cub, an elephant, or a Michelangelo, according to its kind? How does the spider make its web, or the swallows find their way across the seas? These marvels do not astonish us because we are used to them. But we ought to have the courage to admit that, usual as they are, they are none the less mysteries.

The facts of metapsychics are neither more nor less mysterious than the phenomena of electricity, of fertilization, and of heat. They are not so usual; that is the whole difference. But it is absurd to decline to study them because they are unusual . . .

We constantly find that the authors and observers who have busied themselves with metapsychics show a very regrettable tendency to consider only their own observations as exact, and to reject all others. Thus (with certain exceptions) those who have confined their studies exclusively to telepathy and the subjective side of metapsychics are prone to attach excessive importance to that aspect of the facts and to refuse credence to phenomena of telekinesis and ectoplasm, however well substantiated.

This is the case with several eminent members of the English S. P. R. [Society for Psychical Research]. They are easily satisfied in cases of mental transmission, even though that may be sometimes explicable by coincidence; but as soon as physical phenomena are in question they demand impossible proofs even when such proofs are useless to the demonstration.

Conversely, an experimenter, who considers himself to have seen a materialization, will take it as well authenticated, though his study may have been quite superficial; and will put forward exaggerated and ridiculously severe criticisms of transmission of thought or of materializations described by other observers perhaps quite as competent as himself.

When a phenomenon is unusual, even those who are open to new truths do not admit it without personal verification. It seems, however, that our criticism, severe as it may be (and should be), ought to be exercised as much, if not more, upon our own observations than on those of others. If I permit myself to criticize the mentality of scientists towards metapsychic matters, I do so because I have fallen into the same mistake myself. In working at this subject I did not follow the procedure usual in the study of other sciences. I made experiments before studying books; so that I started by acquiring personal convictions, which were not in the least bookish. Only subsequently did I read and meditate on the works of ancient and modern experimentalists who have devoted themselves to such researches. I was then astounded at the volume and the completeness of the proofs. My own experiments and those of others finally led me to a profound conviction that metapsychics is a real science to be treated like all other sciences—laboriously, methodically, and with respect.

These unusual phenomena are real: (1) There is a faculty of cognition other than our usual faculties; (2) there are movements of objects other than those to which we are accustomed.

And it is irrational to refuse to study these unusual phenomena by the methods of observation and experiment that have answered so well in all other sciences. Claude Bernard has differentiated the sciences that rest on observation from those that rest on experiment. Metapsychics belongs to both classes. It is often experimental, like chemistry and physiology; but it is often akin to historical science and rests on human testimony.

Under its experimental aspect it should be treated as an experimental science, by technical methods of research, with scales, photography, by graphic methods—all the devices of exact measurement employed by physiologists. I perceive no essential difference between the proper experimental methods, except that the chemist and the physiologist are dealing with easily procurable materials, whereas the student of metapsychics requires a *medium*, a human subject difficult to find, easily put off his balance, and highly capricious, who must at all times be handled very diplomatically. But once an experiment has begun, it should be carried out as rigorously as one on arterial pressure or on the heat generated by burning acetylene.

In no kind of experiment are all the conditions absolutely within control. This axiom of scientific method applies more strongly in metapsychics than in any other science. Darkness may be necessary, or silence; or perhaps noise? Perhaps some ill-defined psychological conditions may be essential also? After all, this applies to all infant sciences; in their embryonic stage the conditions requisite to the development of the facts to be proved are not known. The experimenter falls into gross mistakes and the experiment fails just when he naïvely imagines that he has provided all the elements of success.

In so far as it is an observational and traditional science, metapsychics has abundant documentary evidence. This is profoundly unequal in value, and it is necessary to know how to choose the material and to separate the wheat from the tares by severe criticism. But to condemn all recorded observation would be irrational; all historical science is derived from such records. Has not medicine up to the time of Claude Bernard and Pasteur been a science of observation? Is it not largely so today? A great physiologist has said that a well-observed fact is as valid as a good experiment. This is perhaps going a little too far, for the certitude given by an observation is of inferior quality to that resulting from a good experiment. Nevertheless, the sciences that rest on observations are valid, and it is folly to wish to reject records.

But there is no need to set the one method in opposition to the other. When observation and experiment lead to the same results, they mutually confirm each other. In this book, therefore, will be found two chapters on each variety of phenomena, one dealing with experiments and the other with observations, whether the matter in hand concerns lucidity (cryptesthesia), the movement of objects (telekinesis), or materializations (ectoplasmic forms).

Experimental method is relatively easy, whereas the method of observation is extremely difficult. The documentary evidence is often doubtful. It is voluminous, far too voluminous; metapsychic science is hampered by imperfect experiments and malobservation. Those who have cultivated it, instead of handling it with scientific exactitude, have treated it as a religion for adepts—an error that has had disastrous results.

Spiritualists have intermingled religion and science to the great detriment of the latter.

Not that I would blame the efforts of spiritualists; that would be gross ingratitude. While official science, followed by the immense majority of the public, rejected disdainfully without examination, and often with obvious ill will, the work of Crookes, A. R. Wallace, and Zöllner, the spiritualists took up the facts and set to work upon them. But instead of making them matters of science, they made them matters of religion. They carried on their séances in a mystical atmosphere, with prayers; speaking of moral regeneration; preoccupied with mysteries; convinced that they were conversing with the dead; and losing themselves in infantile discursiveness. They refused to see that metapsychic facts are of the present, not of the beyond, for perhaps there is no beyond. "The beyond" has been their ruin, and they have lost themselves in puerile theology and theosophy.

When a historian studies the *Capitularies* of Charlemagne, he is not thinking of the beyond; when a physiologist is measuring the muscular contractions of a frog he says nothing about ultraterrestrial spheres; when a chemist determines the amount of nitrogen in lecithin he says nothing about human survival. Metapsychics must be treated after the same manner, without dreams about ethereal worlds or psychic emanations; we must remain on the earth, take all theory soberly, and only consider humbly whether the phenomenon studied is true, without seeking to deduce the mysteries of past or future existences.

For instance, when we are studying cryptesthesia and seeking to discover whether a sensitive will give the name we are thinking of, without any indication on our part, our whole attention should be vigilantly concentrated on giving absolutely no sign whatever, and on comparing the letters given by the subject with those in the name thought of, according to the mathematical probability of 1:25, since there are twenty-five letters in the [French] alphabet . . . If we are studying telekinesis, the limbs of the medium must be held firmly enough to make sure that the table cannot be moved by her hands, her feet, or by any trick [what]soever.

It does not interest me to go beyond this. I am keenly interested in these humble tasks, which need no small courage to undertake, without connecting them with the immortality of the soul.

What valuable observations and marvellous experiments have been distorted and deformed by the constant and dangerous desire of laying the foundations of a new religion! Spiritist religion is inimical to science. I might borrow from the Bible the motto for all our studies: *Omnia in numero et pondere*, says the preacher—an admirable principle, applicable to all science and the very negation of religious mysticism.

If a creed be needed, it is the creed of truth—naked truth—without adornments and without verbiage. Let us verify phenomena, and try to link them together by any theory that has as much verisimilitude as possible, but let us never sacrifice the facts, which are certainly true to the theory, which is probably false.

No doubt metapsychic phenomena often seem to impel us to nebulous inferences as to human immortality, to emanations from an unknown Will, to reincarnation, and to fluidic projections from the living or the dead. I have endeavoured to set aside these premature theories, though I have not been able to do this entirely. What purpose has been served by the ponderous volumes on alchemy before Lavoisier? He did achieve more with his scales than did all the dissertations of Goclenius, Agrippa, and Paracelsus. If we desire that metapsychics should take rank as a science, let us first establish its facts on a solid foundation. Our successors will go further, no doubt, but our duty today is less ambitious; let us have the intellectual modesty that befits our ignorance.

Nevertheless, in certain respects metapsychics cannot be compared with any other science. No intelligence is apparent in the various modes of energy, whereas both in objective and subjective metapsychics the phenomena seem due to some kind of intelligence. The intelligence that pertains to metapsychic things may be purely human; but, if so, it proceeds from a region of human intelligence quite unknown to us, since it reveals things that our senses cannot reveal and acts upon matter otherwise than by muscular contraction. In any case the province of metapsychics differs from that of all other forces, these latter being certainly blind and unconscious. Perhaps it may eventually be proved that the metapsychic forces producing the phenomena are as unconscious as electricity and heat. Then metapsychics will form a branch of physics and psychology. This would be a great advance, and, far from being saddened thereby, we should rather be glad; for there is a real mental intellectual distress, felt by none more than myself, in the supposition that unknown, arbitrary, and capricious powers are the only ones endowed with intelligence.

But this day has not yet dawned and we must conclude provisionally: (1) That the metapsychic facts are real; (2) that they are to be studied like every other science without religious preoccupations, and (3) that they are seemingly directed by human or non-human intelligences whose intentions we can only partially perceive.

Appendix E

~

Bibliography About and by Charles Richet with Emphasis on Psychic Phenomena, compiled by Carlos S. Alvarado, PhD, and Renaud Evrard, PhD

*About Richet's psychic work or **with some information about it.

About Richet

*Alvarado, C.S. (2008). Charles Richet on "The Limits of Psychic and Metapsychic Science." *Psypioneer, 4*, 198-207. Retrieved from http://www.iapsop.com/psypioneer/psypioneer_v4_n9_sep_2008.pdf [Partly reprinted in Chapter 6]

Alvarado, C.S. (2008). Aspects of the history of parapsychology: II. Charles Richet's (1850-1935) work in psychical research. Retrieved from http://www.pflyceum.org/10.html

*Alvarado, C.S. (2008). Note on Charles Richet's "La Suggestion Mentale et le Calcul des Probabilités" (1884). *Journal of Scientific Exploration, 22,* 543–548. [Partly reprinted in Chapter 2]

*Alvarado, C.S. (2010). Review of *Traité de Métapsychique,* by C. Richet. *Journal of Scientific Exploration, 24,* 535–541. [Partly reprinted in Chapter 5]

*Alvarado, C.S. (2011). Upholding Psychical Research in Front of Psychologists: An Excerpt from a Paper by Charles Richet at the Fifth International Congress of Psychology (Rome, 1905). *Psypioneer Journal, 7*(3), 79–88. Retrieved from http://www.iapsop.com/psypioneer/psypioneer_v7_n3_mar_2011.pdf [Partly reprinted in Chapter 4]

*Alvarado, C.S. (2012). Charles Richet on mediumship and the unconscious. *Mindfield, 4*(1), 27–28.

*Alvarado, C.S. (2015). Charles Richet on Leonora Piper [Letter to the Editor]. *Journal of the Society for Psychical Research, 79,* 56–59. [Reprinted in Appendix A]

*Alvarado, C.S. (2016). Charles Richet. In R. McLuhan (Ed.), *Psi Encyclopedia.* London: Society for Psychical Research. Retrieved from http://psi.circle-interactive.co.uk/articles/charles-richet [Reprinted in Chapter 1]

*Alvarado, C.S. (2016). Richet's Traité de Métapsychique (Thirty Years of Psychical Research). In R. McLuhan (Ed.), *Psi Encyclopedia.* London: Society for Psychical Research. Retrieved from http://psi-encyclopedia.spr.ac.uk/book-reviews/richets-traite-de-metapsychique-thirty-years-of-psychical-research

*Alvarado, C.S. (2016). Richet's 'La Suggestion Mentale.' In R. McLuhan (Ed.), *Psi Encyclopedia.*

London: Society for Psychical Research. Retrieved from http://psi-encyclopedia.spr.ac.uk/articles/richets-la-suggestion-mentale

**Alvarado, C.S. (2017). Telepathy, mediumship and psychology: Psychical research at the international congresses of psychology, 1889–1905. *Journal of Scientific Exploration, 31,* 255–292.

*Alvarado, C.S. (2018). Fragments of a life in psychical research: The case of Charles Richet. *Journal of Scientific Exploration, 32,* 61–84. [Partly reprinted in Chapter 2]

*Alvarado, C.S., & Evrard, R. (2012). The psychic sciences in France: Historical notes on the *Annales des sciences psychiques. Journal of Scientific Exploration, 26,* 117-140.

*Amadou, R. (1957). Charles Richet—His life and work. *Tomorrow, 5*(5), 66–80.

**Brower, M.B. (2010). *Unruly Spirits: The Science of Psychic Phenomena in Modern France.* Urbana, IL: University of Illinois Press.

**Carbonel, F. (2008). Au-delà de Paris et Nancy, l' "Ecole de Charles Richet" selon Pierre Janet: Son impact et ses réseaux, ses membres et son hétérodoxie de l'appel à un Congrès International de Psychologie (1881) à la fondation d'un Institut Psychique (1900). *Janetian Studies, 5,* Retrieved from http://halshs.archives-ouvertes.fr/halshs-00288437

**Carroy, J. (2004). Playing with signatures: The young Charles Richet. In M.S. Micale (Ed.), *The Mind of Modernism: Medicine, Psychology, and the Cultural Arts in Europe and America, 1880–1940* (pp. 217–249). Stanford, CA: Stanford University Press.

*Edelman, N. (2007). Charles Richet, le Nobel qui voulait comprendre le paranormal. *Revue du Praticien,* 57, 689–693.

**Estingoy, P. (1993). *Charles Richet, Esquisse Biographique et Bibliographique.* Mémoire de DEA d'Histoire, Université Lyon III.

*Evrard, R. (2016). *La Légende de l'Esprit: Enquête sur 150 Ans de Parapsychologie.* Paris: Trajectoire.

**Evrard, R., Gumpper, S., Beauvis, B., & Alvarado, C.S. (in press). "Never sacrifice anything to laboratory work": The "physiological psychology" of Charles Richet (1875-1905). *Journal of the History of the Behavioral Sciences.*

*Gasperini, L. (2011). Criptestesia o ipotesi spiritica? Ch. Richet ed E. Bozzano a confronto. *Luce e Ombra,* 111, 113–126.

**Lachapelle, S. (2011). *Investigating the Supernatural: From Spiritism and Occultism to Psychical Research and Metapsychics in France, 1853–1931.* Baltimore: Johns Hopkins University Press.

*Le Maléfan, P. (2004). La psychopathologie confrontée aux fantômes: L'épisode de la villa Carmen: Contribution à l'histoire marginale de la psychologie et de la psychopathologie. https://sites.google.com/site/psychologieethistoire/autresrevuesd%27histoire23222

*Magalhães, S.N. (2007). *Charles Richet: O Apóstolo da Ciência e o Espiritismo.* Rio de Janeiro, Brazil: Federação Espírita Brasileira.

**Marmin, N. (2001). Métapsychique et psychologie en France (1880–1940). *Revue d'Histoire des Sciences Humaines,* 4(1), 145–171. (For a more complete account see Marmin,

N. (2001). *La Métapsychique (1875-1935). Une Impasse Fructueuse dans l'Histoire de la Science de l'Esprit.* Thèse d'histoire de la psychologie, Paris : Université Paris V.)

**Monroe, J.W. (2008). *Laboratories of Faith. Mesmerism, Spiritism, and Occultism in Modern France.* Ithaca, NY: Cornell University Press.

** Osty, E. (1936). Charles Richet (1850-1935). *Revue Métapsychique*, No. 1, 1–42.

*Pierson, J. (1940). Charles Richet (1850–1935): His attitude an influence on psychical research in Europe. *Journal of the American Society for Psychical Research, 35,* 173–183..

**Plas, R. (2000). *Naissance d'une Science Humaine: La Psychologie: Les Psychologues et le "Merveilleux Psychique".* Rennes: Presses Universitaires de Rennes.

** Richet, C. (1917). *Mémoires sur Moi et les Autres: Vol. 4: Mes Années d'Agrégé (1878-1887).* Unpublished, Bibliothèque de l'Académie de médecine, Paris.

*Tabori, P. (1972). *Pioneers of the Unseen.* London: Souvenir Press.

*Tocquet, R. (1969). Charles Richet. *Revue Métapsychique*, No. 14, 9–17.

**Van Wijland, J. (Ed.). (2015). *Charles Richet (1850-1935): L'Exercice de la Curiosité.* Renne: Presses Universitaires de Rennes.

*Warcollier, R. (1959). Our pioneers: VII: Charles Richet (1850-1935). *Journal of the Society for Psychical Research, 40,* 157–162.

**Wolf, S. (1993). *Brain, Mind and Medicine: Charles Richet and the Origins of Physiological Psychology.* New Brunswick: Transaction Publishers.

By Richet

Includes related matters such as hypnosis and changes of personality.

Geley, G., & Richet, C. (1922). À propos des expériences de la Sorbonne. *Revue Métapsychique*, No. 4, 225-230.

Richet, C. (1875). Du somnambulisme provoqué. *Journal de l'Anatomie et de la Physiologie Normales et Pathologiques de l'Homme et des Animaux, 11*, 348–378.

Richet, C. (1880). Les démoniaques d'aujourd'hui. *Revue des Deux Mondes, 37*, 340–372, 552–583, 828–863.

Richet, C. (1880). Du somnambulisme provoqué. *Revue Philosophique de la France et de l'Étranger, 10*, 337–374, 462–484.

Richet, C. (1883). La personnalité et la mémoire dans le somnambulisme. *Revue Philosophique de la France et de l'Étranger, 15*, 225–242.

Richet, C. (1884). *L'Homme et l'Intelligence: Fragments de Physiologie et de Psychologie.* Paris: Félix Alcan.

Richet, C. (1884). Note on mental suggestion. *Brain, 7*, 83–85.

Richet, C. (1884). À propos de la suggestion mentale. *Compte Rendus Hebdomadaires de Séances et Mémoires de la Société de Biologie, 1*(s. 8), 365–367.

Richet, C. (1884). La suggestion mentale et le calcul des probabilités. *Revue Philosophique de la France et de l'Étranger, 18*, 609–674.

Richet, C, (1885). Des rapports de l'hallucination avec l'état mental. *Revue Philosophique de la France et de l'Étranger, 20*, 333–335.

Richet, C. (1886). L'action des substances toxiques et médicamenteuses à distance. *Revue Philosophique de la France et de l'Étranger, 21,* 321-323.

Richet, C. (1886). Un fait de somnambulisme à distance. *Revue Philosophique de la France et de l'Étranger, 21,* 199–200.

Richet, C. (1886). Les mouvements inconscients. In M. Berthelot (Ed.), *Hommage à Monsieur Chevreul a l'Occasion de son Centenaire 31 Aout 1886* (pp. 79–84). Paris: Félix Alcan.

Richet, C. (1886). De quelques phénomènes de suggestion sans hypnotisme. *Revue Philosophique de la France et de l'Étranger, 21,* 324–326.

Richet, C. (1887). Préface de M. Ch. Richet. In J. Ochorowicz, *De la Suggestion Mentale* (pp. i– v). Paris; Octave Doin.

Richet, C. (1887). Sommeil à distance. *Journal of the Society for Psychical Research, 3,* 150-152.

Richet, C. (1888). Expériences sur le sommeil à distance. *Revue Philosophique de la France et de l'Étranger, 25,* 435–452. [See also *Revue de l'Hypnotisme Expérimental et Thérapeutique, 2,* 225-240]

Richet, C. (1888). Recent experiments by M. Charles Richet on telepathic hypnotism. *Journal of the Society for Psychical Research, 3,* 222–226. [Summary of paper by Richet]

Richet, C. (1888). Relation de diverses expériences sur la transmission mentale, la lucidité, et autres phénomènes non explicables par les données scientifiques actuelles. *Proceedings of the Society for Psychical Research, 5,* 18–168.

Richet, C. (1889). Further experiments in hypnotic lucidity or clairvoyance. *Proceedings of the Society for Psychical Research, 6*, 66–83.

Richet, C. (1890). Les hallucinations télépathiques. *Revue Scientifique, 46*, 784–787.

Richet, C. (1890). Les travaux du Congrès de Psychologie Physiologique. *Congrès International de Psychologie Physiologique* (pp. 32–38). Paris: Bureau de Revues.

Richet, C. (1891). *Experimentelle Studien auf dem Gebiete der Gedankenübertragung und des sogenannten Hellsehens.* Stuttgart: Enke.

Richet, C. (1891). Des phénomènes psychiques: Lettre à M. Dariex. *Annales des Sciences Psychiques, 1*, 1–8.

Richet, C. (1891). Préface. In E. Gurney, F.W.H. Myers, & F. Podmore, *Les Hallucinations Télépathiques* (pp. v–xiii). Paris: Félix Alcan.

Richet, C. (1892). L'avenir de la psychologie. *International Congress of Experimental Psychology* (pp. 24–26). London: Williams & Norgate.

Richet, C. (1892). L'avenir de la psychologie. *Annales des Sciences Psychiques, 2*, 341–350.

Richet, C. (1892). À propos du mysticisme moderne: Réplique a M. Rosenbach. *Annales des Sciences Psychiques, 2*, 293–301.

Richet, C. (1893). Expériences de Milan. *Annales des Sciences Psychiques, 3*, 1–31.

Richet, C. (1893). Le hasard et la probabilité: Note relative aux expériences de M. Roux. *Annales des Sciences Psychiques, 3*, 209–211.

Richet, C. (1895). À propos des expériences faites avec Eusapia Paladino: Réponse à M. Hodgson. *Journal of the Society for Psychical Research, 7*, 67–75.

Richet, C. (1899). On the conditions of certainty. *Proceedings of the Society for Psychical Research, 14*, 152–157.

Richet, C. (1900). Un cas remarquable de précocité musicale. *Annales des Sciences Psychiques, 10*, 324–331.

Richet, C. (1901). In memoriam Frederic W.H. Myers. *Annales des Sciences Psychiques, 11*, 173–178.

Richet, C. (1902). Occultisme dans l'antiquité. *Annales des Sciences Psychiques, 12*, 310–312.

Richet, C. (1903). Étude sur un cas de prémonition. *Annales des Sciences Psychiques, 13*, 65–71.

Richet, C. (1903). Préface. In J. Maxwell, *Les Phénomènes Psychiques* (pp. vii–xi). Paris: Félix Alcan.

Richet, C. (1905). Concerning the phenomenon called materialisation. *Annals of Psychical Science, 2*, 207–210, 269–289.

Richet, C. (1905). The decimal indexing of memoranda relating to psychical sciences. *Annals of Psychical Sciences, 1*, 69–74.

Richet, C. (1905). Metapsychical phenomena of by-gone times. *Annals of Psychical Sciences, 1*, 207–229.

Richet, C. (1905). La métapsychique. *Proceedings of the Society for Psychical Research, 19*, 2–49.

Richet, C. (1905). Personality and changes of personality. *Annals of Psychical Sciences, 1*, 273–297.

Richet, C. (1905). Should the phenomena of spiritism be seriously studied? *Annals of Psychical Sciences, 1,* 5–46.

Richet, C. (1905). On a singular case of lucidity. *Annals of Psychical Sciences, 1,* 130–135.

Richet, C. (1905). Xénoglossie: L'écriture automatique en langues étrangères. *Proceedings of the Society for Psychical Research, 19,* 162–194.

Richet, C. (1905). Xenoglossy: Or automatic writing in foreign languages. *Annals of Psychical Sciences, 1,* 337–373.

Richet, C. (1906). L'avenir de la psychologie. In S. De Sanctis (Ed.), *Atti del V Congresso Internazionale di Psicologia* (pp. 166–173). Rome: Forzani.

Richet, C. (1906). The future of psychology. *Annals of Psychical Science, 4,* 201–216.

Richet, C. (1906). Nachschrift Red. *Psychische Studien, 33,* 207-211.

Richet, C. (1906). *Les Phénomènes dits de Matérialisation de la villa Carmen (avec Documents Nouveaux et Discussions).* Paris: Félix Alcan.

Richet, C. (1907). "Metapsychism" or "occultism"? *Annals of Psychical Science, 6,* 423–425.

Richet, C. (1908). An enquiry into premonitions. *Annals of Psychical Science, 7,* 24–26.

Richet, C. (1908). Des limites de l'incrédulite. *Annales des Sciences Psychiques, 18,* 97–101.

Richet, C. (1909). My experiments with Mme. X. *Annals of Psychical Science, 8,* 1–145.

Richet, C. (1909). Occultism in antiquity: Plutarch. *Annals of Psychical Science, 8,* 207–208.

Richet, C. (1914). L'éloge de la raison. *Annales des Sciences Psychiques, 24,* 79–81.

Richet, C. (1917). Avez-vous eu des pressentiments? *Bulletin des Armées de la République Réservé à la Zone des Armées. 4*(266), 4.

Richet, C. (1919). Lucidité. *Annales des Sciences Psychiques, 29,* 49–53.

Richet, C. (1920). Les prémonitions. *Bulletin de l'Institut Métapsychique International,* No. 1, 18–26, No. 2, 74–80.

Richet, C. (1921). L'hypothèse spirite. *Revue Métapsychique,* No. 6, 389–398.

Richet, C. (1921). Riddle of the future: Modern psychical research leaves the question of immortality still unsolved. *New York Times,* October 16, 82.

Richet, C. (1921). Préface. In R. Warcollier, *La Télépathie: Recherches Expérimentales* (pp. v-x). Paris: Félix Alcan.

Richet, C., Santoliquido, R., & de Gramont, A. (1922). La campagne d'injures et de mensonges: Réponses à M. Nordmann. *Revue Métapsychique,* No. 6, 353.

Richet, C. (1922). Un dernier mot sur la cryptesthésie, lucidité: Réponse à M. Bozzano. *Revue Métapsychique,* No. 6, 382–384.

Richet, C. (1922). Expériences décisives de cryptesthésie (lucidité). *Revue Métapsychique,* No. 3, 158–167.

Richet, C. (1922). L'hypothèse de l'hyperesthésie tactile dans les expériences d'Ossowiecki. *Revue Métapsychique,* No. 5, 299–300.

Richet, C. (1922). L'hypothèse spirite: Réponse à Sir Oliver Lodge. *Revue Métapsychique*, No. 3, 153–157.

Richet, C. (1922). De la théorie spirite—Réponse a M. Bozzano. *Revue Métapsychique*, No. 6, 366–371.

Richet, C. (1922). Un dernier mot sur la cryptesthésie–Réponse a M. E. Bozzano. *Revue Métapsychique*, No. 6, 382–384.

Richet, C. (1922). À propos des ectoplasmes. *Revue Métapsychique*, No. 5, 281–283.

Richet, C. (1922). *Traité de Métapsychique*. Paris: Félix Alcan.

Richet, C. (1923). Chez Victor Hugo. *Revue Métapsychique*, No. 3, 137–152.

Richet, C. (1923). Extra-sensorial channels of knowledge and the experimental method. *Lancet*, 2, 493–497.

Richet, C. (1923). *Grundriss der Parapsychologie und der Parapsychophysik*. Stuttgart: Union Deutsche Verlagsgesellschaft.

Richet, C. (1923). Réponse à M. P. Janet: À propos de métapsychique. *Revue Philosophique de la France et de l'Etranger*, 96, 462–471.

Richet, C. (1923). *Thirty Years of Psychical Research*. New York: Macmillan. (Translated from the second French edition of *Traité de Métapsychique*, 1922)

Richet, C. (1924). For and against survival: The difficulty of survival from the scientific point of view. *Proceedings of the Society for Psychical Research, 34*, 107–113.

Richet, C. (1924). La défense de la métapsychique: Réponse au Docteur Achille Delmas. *Revue Métapsychique*, No. 1, 5–16.

Richet, C. (1924). L'écriture "presque" automatique. *Revue Métapsychique*, No. 2, 135–137.

Richet, C. (1924). Metapsychic science and survival. *Journal of the Society for Psychical Research, 21*, 274–278.

Richet, C. (1924). Préface. In *L'État Actuel des Recherches Psychiques d'Après les Travaux du IIme Congrès International Tenu à Varsovie en 1923 en l'Honneur du Dr Julien Ochorowicz*. Paris: Presses Universitaires de France.

Richet, C. (1925). Camille Flammarion. *Revue Métapsychique*, No. 3, 129–131.

Richet, C. (1925). La danse automatique. *Revue Métapsychique*, No. 1, 37–38.

Richet, C. (1925). Préface. In A. de Schrenck-Notzing, *Les Phénomènes Physiques de la Médiumnité*. Paris: Payot.

Richet, C. (1925). La science métapsychique. *La Presse Médicale, 33*, 857–862.

Richet, C. (1926). Une critique inopérante: M. Albert Moll et la cryptesthésie de Khan. *Revue Métapsychique*, No. 3, 215–218.

Richet, C. (1926). Un problème de biologie génèrale: À propos de nouvelles experiences de crytesthésie. *Revue Métapsychique*, No. 1, 26–27.

Richet, C. (1927). La métapsychique science nouvelle. *Le Journal*, September 26, 1.

Richet, C. (1927). [Untitled]. In F. Divoire (Ed.), *Les Miracles de la Volonté* (pp. 59-64). Paris: Montaigne.

Richet, C. (1928). *Notre Sixième Sens*. Paris: Montaigne.

Richet, C. (1930). Prefazione. In E. Servadio, *La Ricerca Psichica*. Rome: Cremonese.

Richet, C. (1931). Les rayons cosmiques. *Revue Métapsychique*, No. 3, 208–209.

Richet, C. (1933). *La Grande Espérance*. Paris: Montaigne.

Richet, C. (1933). Pour le progrès de la métapsychique. *Revue Métapsychique*, No. 6, 345–346.

Richet, C. (1933). *Souvenirs d'un Physiologiste*. Paris: J. Peyronnet. (Chapter 20)

Richet, C. (1934). Un fait de prémonition au XVII siècle. *Revue Métapsychique*, No. 4, 261.

Richet, C. (1934). Lucidité et probabilité: Une expérience de Forthuny. *Revue Métapsychique*, No. 4, 256–260.

Richet, C. (1934). Une prémonition remarquable. *Revue Métapsychique*, No. 4, 321.

Richet, C. (1935). *Au Secours!* Paris: J. Peyronnet.

Richet, C. (n.d., ca 1931). *L'Avenir et la Prémonition*. Paris: Montaigne.

Richet, C. (n.d., ca 1929). *Our Sixth Sense*. London: Rider. (First published in French, 1928)

Appendix F

~

Bibliography About the History of Psychical Research and Related Areas

Alvarado, C.S. (2002). Dissociation in Britain during the late nineteenth century: The Society for Psychical Research, 1882-1900. *Journal of Trauma and Dissociation, 3,* 9–33.

Alvarado, C.S. (2010). Classic text No. 84: 'Divisions of personality and spiritism' by Alfred Binet (1896). *History of Psychiatry, 21,* 487–500.

Alvarado, C.S. (2016). On psychic forces and doubles: The case of Albert de Rochas. *Journal of Scientific Exploration, 30,* 63–84.

Alvarado, C.S., & Biondi, M. (2017). Classic Text No. 110: Cesare Lombroso on mediumship and pathology. *History of Psychiatry, 28,* 225–241.

Alvarado, C.S., & Evrard, R. (2012). The psychic sciences in France: Historical notes on the *Annales des Sciences Psychiques. Journal of Scientific Exploration, 26,* 117–140.

Alvarado, C.S., & Evrard, R. (2013). Nineteenth century psychical research in mainstream journals: The *Revue Philosophique de la France et de l'Étranger. Journal of Scientific Exploration, 27,* 655–689.

Alvarado, C.S., & Krippner, S. (2010). Nineteenth century pioneers in the study of dissociation: William James and psychical research. *Journal of Consciousness Studies, 17,* 19–43.

Alvarado, C.S., & Zingrone, N.L. (2012). Classic Text No. 90: 'The Pathology and Treatment of Mediomania', by Frederic Rowland Marvin (1874). *History of Psychiatry, 23,* 229–244.

Anderson, R. I. (1990). Robert Hare's contribution to psychical research. *Journal of the American Society for Psychical Research, 84,* 235–262.

Asprem, E. (2010). A nice arrangement of heterodoxies: William McDougall and the professionalization of psychical research. *Journal of the History of the Behavioral Sciences, 46,* 123–143.

Bauer, E. (1967). Max Dessoir und die Parapsychologie als Wissenschaft. *Zeitschrift für Parapsychologie und Grenzgebiete der Psychologie, 10,* 106–114.

Beloff, J. (1993). *Parapsychology: A Concise History.* London: Athlone Press.

Bensaude-Vincent, B., & Blondel, C. (Eds.). (2002). *Des Savants Face à l'Occulte 1870-1940.* Paris: La Découverte.

Berger, A.S. (1988). *Lives and Letters in American Parapsychology: A Biographical History, 1850-1987.* Jefferson, NC: McFarland.

Biondi, M. (1983). Giovanni Battista Ermacora e la ricerca psichica. *Luce e Ombra, 83,* 177–188.

Biondi, M. (1988). *Tavoli e Medium: Storia dello Spiritismo in Italia.* Rome: Gremese.

Biondi, M. (1993). Mendeleev e le commissioni di indagine sullo spiritismo. *Luce e Ombra, 93,* 62–70.

Biondi, M. (1994). Tentativi di ricerca psichica tra Ottocento e Novecento. *Quaderni di Parapsicologia, 25,* 11–26.

Biondi, M. (2009). Marco Levi Bianchini: A forgotten Italian supporter of parapsychology. *Journal of Scientific Exploration, 23,* 323–328.

Blum, D. (2006). *Ghost Hunters: William James and the Search for Scientific Proof of Life After Death.* New York: Penguin Press.

Brancaccio, M.T. (2014). Enrico Morselli's *Psychology and "Spiritism":* Psychiatry, psychology and psychical research in Italy in the decades around 1900. *Studies in History and Philosophy of Biological and Biomedical Sciences, 48,* 75–84.

Bringmann, W.G., Bringmann, N.J., & Bauer, E. (1990). Fechner und die Parapsychologie. *Zeitschrift für Parapsychologie und Grenzgebiete der Psychologie, 32,* 19–43.

Caratelli, G., & Felici, M.L. (2011). An important subject at the Institut Métapsychique International: Jeanne Laplace: The 1927–1934 experiments. *Journal of Scientific Exploration, 25,* 479–495.

Coon, D.J. (1992). Testing the limits of sense and science: American experimental psychologists combat spiritualism, 1880-1920. *American Psychologist, 47,* 143–151.

Chéroux, C., Fischer, A., Apraxine, P., Canguilhen, D., & Schmit, S. (2005). *The Perfect Medium: Photography and the Occult.* New Haven and London: Yale University Press.

Crabtree, A. (1994). *From Mesmer to Freud: Magnetic Sleep and the Roots of Psychological Healing.* New Haven, CT: Yale University Press.

Delorme, S. (2014). Physiology or psychic powers? William Carpenter and the debate over spiritualism in Victorian Britain. *Studies in History and Philosophy of Science, 48,* 57–66.

Dening, T.R. (1994). Death-coincidences or wishful thinking? The Society for Psychical Research and the 1894 Census of Hallucinations. *History of Psychiatry, 5,* 397–416.

Dèttore, U. (1976). *Storia della Parapsicologia.* Milano: Armenia.

Dingwall, E.J. (Ed.) (1967–1968). *Abnormal Hypnotic Phenomena: A Survey of Nineteenth-Century Cases.* (4 vols.). London: J. &. J. Churchill.

Evrard, R. (2009). René Sudre (1880-1968): The metapsychist's quill. *Journal of the Society for Psychical Research, 73,* 207–222.

Evrard, R. (2011). Cuando el Premio Nobel Pierre Curie se encontró con la médium Eusapia Palladino. *E-Boletín Psi, 6*(1), 3–12.

Evrard, R. (2016). *Enquête sur 150 Ans de Parapsychologie: La Légende de l'Esprit.* Escalquens, France: Trajectoire.

Evrard, R., & Pratte, E.A. (2017). From catalepsy to psychical research: The itinerary of Timothée Puel (1812-1890). *History of Psychology, 20,* 50–71.

Evrard, R., Pratte, E.A., & Cardeña, E. (2018). Pierre Janet and the enchanted boundary of psychical research. *History of Psychology, 21,* 100–125.

Gasperini, L. (2011). Ernesto Bozzano: An Italian spiritualist and psychical researcher. *Journal of Scientific Exploration, 25,* 755–773.

Gauld, A. (1968). *The Founders of Psychical Research.* London: Routledge & Kegan Paul.

Gauld, A. (1978). Psychical research in Cambridge from the seventeenth century to the present. *Journal of the Society for Psychical Research, 49,* 925–937.

Gauld, A. (1992). *A History of Hypnotism.* Cambridge: Cambridge University Press.

Gissurarson, L.R., & Haraldsson, E. (2001). History of parapsychology in Iceland. *International Journal of Parapsychology, 12,* 29–51.

Gonçalves, V.P., & Ortega, F. (2013). Uma nosologia para os fenômenos sobrenaturais e a construção do cérebro "possuído" no século XIX. *Historia, Ciências, Saude-Manguinhos, 20,* 373–390.

Gregory, A. (1985). *The Strange Case of Rudi Schneider.* Metuchen, NJ: Scarecrow Press.

Gutierez, G., & Maillard, N (2005). *Les Aventuriers de l'Esprit.* Paris: Presses du Châtelet.

Gyimesi, J. (2012). Sándor Ferenczi and the problem of telepathy. *History of the Human Sciences, 25,* 131–148.

Hacking, I. (1988). Telepathy: Origins of randomization in experimental design. *Isis, 70,* 427–251.

Hamilton, T. (2009). *Immortal Longings: F.W.H. Myers and the Victorian Search for Life After Death.* Exeter: Imprint Academic.

Haraldsson, E., & Gissurarson, L. (2015). *Indridi Indridason: The Icelandic Physical Medium.* Hove, UK: White Crow Books.

Iannuzzo, G. (1983) *Ernesto Bozzano: La Vita e l'Opera* (Le Monografie di Luce e Ombra, No. 2). Verona: Luce e Ombra.

Iannuzzo, G. (1986). Psichiatri e spiriti: La psichiatria italiana degli inizi del '900 e la ricerca psichica. *Quaderni di Parapsicologia, 17,* 111–125.

Inglis, B. (1984). *Science and Parascience: A History of the Paranormal, 1914–1939.* London: Hodder and Stoughton.

Inglis, B. (1992). *Natural and Supernatural: A History of the Paranormal from Earliest Times to 1914* (rev. ed.). Dorset: Prism.

Junior, A.S., Araujo, S. de F., & Moreira-Almeida, A. (2013). William James and psychical research: Towards a radical science of mind. *History of Psychiatry, 24,* 62–78.

Kelly, E. F. (2001). The contributions of F.W.H. Myers to psychology. *Journal of the Society for Psychical Research, 65,* 65–90.

Knapp, K.D. (2017). *William James: Psychical Research and the Challenge of Modernity.* Chapel Hill: University of North Carolina Press.

Lachapelle, S. (2011). *Investigating the Supernatural: From Spiritism and Occultism to Psychical Research and Metapsychics in France, 1853–1931.* Baltimore: Johns Hopkins University Press.

Lamont, P. (2005). *The First Psychic: The Peculiar Mystery of a Notorious Victorian Wizard.* London: Little Brown.

Le Maléfan, P. (1999). *Folie et Spiritisme: Histoire du Discourse Psychopathologique sur la Pratique du Spiritisme, ses Abords et ses Avatars (1850–1950).* Paris: L'Hartmattan,

Le Maléfan, P., & Sommer, A. (2015). Léon Marillier and the veridical hallucination in late-nineteenth- and early-twentieth-century French psychology and psychopathology. *History of Psychiatry, 26,* 418–432.

Luckhurst, R. (2002). *The Invention of Telepathy 1870-1901.* Oxford: Oxford University Press.

Maraldi, E. de O., & Alvarado, C.S. (2018). Classic Text No. 113: Final chapter, From India to the Planet Mars: A Study of a Case of Somnambulism with Glossolalia, by Théodore Flournoy (1900). *History of Psychiatry, 29,* 110–125.

Mauskopf, S.H., & McVaugh, M.R. (1980). *The Elusive Science: Origins of Experimental Psychical Research.* Baltimore: Johns Hopkins University Press.

McCorristine, S (2010). *Spectres of the Self: Thinking about Ghosts and Ghost-Seeing in England, 1750–1920.* Cambridge: Cambridge University Press.

Méheust, B. (1999). *Somnambulisme et Mediumnité (1784-1930)* (2 vols.). Le Plessis-Robinson: Institut Synthélabo pour de Progrès de la Connaissance.

Monroe, J. W. (2008). *Laboratories of Faith: Mesmerism, Spiritism and Occultism in Modern France.* Ithaca: Cornell University Press.

Moreman, C.M. (Ed.). (2013). *The Spiritualist Movement: Speaking with the Dead in America and Around the World* (3 vols.). Santa Barbara, CA: Praeger.

Mülberger, A. (Ed.). (2016). *Los Límites de la Ciencia: Espiritismo, Hipnotismo y el Estudio de los Fenómenos Paranormales (1850–1930).* Madrid: Consejo Superior de Investigaciones Científicas.

Noakes, R. (2004). The "bridge which is between physical and psychical research": William Fletcher Barrett, sensitive flames, and spiritualism. *History of Science, 42,* 419–464.

Noakes, R. (2014). Haunted thoughts of the careful experimentalist: Psychical research and the troubles of experimental physics. *Studies in History and Philosophy of Biological and Biomedical Sciences, 48,* 46–56.

Noakes, R. (2019). *Physics and Psychics: The Occult and the Sciences in Modern Britain.* Cambridge: Cambridge University Press.

Oppenheim, J. (1985). *The Other World: Spiritualism and Psychical Research in England, 1850-1914.* New York: Cambridge University Press.

Parot, F. (1993). Psychology experiments: Spiritism at the Sorbonne. *Journal of the History of the Behavioral Sciences, 29,* 22–28.

Parra, A. (1993). *Historia de la Parapsicología en la Argentina* (2nd ed.). Buenos Aires: Ediciones Monográficas Argentinas.

Plas, R. (2000). *Naissance d'une Science Humaine: La Psychologie: Les Psychologues et le "Merveilleux Psychique."* Rennes: Presses Universitaires de Rennes.

Podmore, F. (1902). *Modern Spiritualism: A History and a Criticism* (2 vols). London: Methuen.

Rabeyron, T., & Evrard, R. (2012). Perspectives historiques et contemporaines sur l'occulte dans la correspondance Freud-Ferenczi. *Recherches en Psychanalyse,* No. 13, 97–111.

Shamdasani, S. (1993). Automatic writing and the discovery of the unconscious. *Spring, 54,* 100–131.

Sommer, A. (2009). From astronomy to transcendental Darwinism: Carl du Prel (1839–1899). *Journal of Scientific Exploration, 23,* 59–68.

Sommer, A. (2009). Tackling taboos—From Psychopathia Sexualis to the materialization of dreams: Albert von-Schrenck-Notzing (1862–1929). *Journal of Scientific Exploration, 23,* 299–322.

Sommer, A. (2011). Professional heresy: Edmund Gurney (1847–1888) and the study of hallucinations and hypnotism. *Medical History, 55,* 383–388.

Sommer, A. (2012). Normalizing the supernormal: The formation of the "Gesellschaft fur Psychologische Forschung ("Society for Psychological Research"), C. 1886–1890. *Journal of the History of the Behavioral Sciences, 49,* 1–26.

Sommer, A. (2012). Psychical research and the origins of American psychology: Hugo Münsterberg, William James and Eusapia Palladino. *History of the Human Sciences, 25,* 23–44.

Sommer, A. (2013). *Crossing the Boundaries of Mind and Body: Psychical Research and the Origins of Modern Psychology.* Ph.D. thesis, University College of London.

Sommer, A. (2013). Spiritualism and the origins of modern Psychology in late nineteenth-century Germany: The Wundt-Zöllner Debate. In C.M. Moreman (Ed.), *The Spiritualist Movement: Speaking with the Dead in America and Around the World* (Vol. 1, pp. 55–72). Santa Barbara, CA: Praeger.

Taves, A. (2014). A tale of two congresses: The psychological study of psychical, occult, and religious phenomena, 1900-1909. *Journal of the History of the Behavioral Sciences, 50,* 376–399.

Tischner, R. (1960). *Geschichte der Parapsychology.* Tittmoning: Walter Pustet.

Treitel, C. (2004). *A Science for the Soul: Occultism and the Genesis of the German Modern.* Baltimore: John Hopkins University Press.

Villanueva, J. (2001). The work of Eugène Osty in psychical research. *International Journal of Parapsychology, 12,* 27–42.

Wolffram, H. (2009). *The Stepchildren of Science: Psychical Research and Parapsychology in Germany, c. 1870–1939.* Amsterdam: Rodopi.

Zingrone, N. L., & Alvarado, C. S. (1987). Historical aspects of parapsychological terminology. *Journal of Parapsychology, 51,* 49–74.

Zingrone, N.L., & Alvarado, C.S. (2015). A brief history of psi research. In E.C May & S.B. Marwaha (Eds.), *Extrasensory Perception: Support, Skepticism, and Science: Vol. 1: History, Controversy, and Research* (pp. 35–79). Santa Barbara, CA: Praeger.

Acknowledgements

~

I would like to thank Nancy L. Zingrone for editorial assistance and for the preparation of the manuscript for publication. Thanks are also due to the editors of the following publications for granting me permission to use previously published material in this book.

(2008). Charles Richet on "The Limits of Psychic and Metapsychic Science." *Psypioneer, 4,* 198–207. Retrieved from http://www.iapsop.com/psypioneer/psypioneer_v4_n9_sep_2008.pdf (Chapter 6)

(2008). Note on Charles Richet's "La Suggestion Mentale et le Calcul des Probabilités" (1884). *Journal of Scientific Exploration, 22,* 543–548. (Chapter 3)

(2010). Review of *Traité de Métapsychique,* by C. Richet. *Journal of Scientific Exploration, 24,* 535–541. (Chapter 5)

(2011). Upholding psychical research in front of psychologists: An excerpt from a paper by Charles Richet at the Fifth International Congress of Psychology (Rome, 1905). *Psypioneer Journal, 7,* 79–88. Retrieved from http://www.iapsop.com/psypioneer/psypioneer_v7_n3_mar_2011.pdf (Chapter 4)

(2015) Charles Richet on Leonora Piper [Letter to the Editor]. *Journal of the Society for Psychical Research, 79,* 56–59. (Appendix A)

(2017). Charles Richet. In R. McLuhan (Ed.), *Psi Encyclopedia.* London: Society for Psychical Research. Retrieved from http://psi.circle-interactive.co.uk/articles/charles-richet (Chapter 1)

(2018). Fragments of a life in psychical research: The case of Charles Richet. *Journal of Scientific Exploration, 32,* 61–84. (Chapter 2)

The chapters in this book were slightly changed for publication

Chapter 2

I wish to thank Renaud Evrard for various suggestions and references to improve this chapter. Massimo Biondi provided me with some information about Italian researchers mentioned in the footnotes, and Nancy L. Zingrone offered numerous useful editorial suggestions.

Appendix A

I wish to thank the Society for Psychical Research for funding the publication of these remarks.

References

~

Introduction

Alvarado, C.S. (2002). Dissociation in Britain during the late nineteenth century: The Society for Psychical Research, 1882–1900. *Journal of Trauma and Dissociation, 3*, 9–33.

Carroy, J. (2004). Playing with signatures: The young Charles Richet. In M.S. Micale (Ed.), *The Mind of Modernism: Medicine, Psychology, and the Cultural Arts in Europe and America, 1880–1940* (pp. 217–249). Stanford, CA: Stanford University Press.

Gauld, A. (1968). *The Founders of Psychical Research.* London: Routledge & Kegan Paul.

Painlevé, P. (1926). Le jubilé de M. Charles Richet. *Le Matin,* May 22, 1.

Plas, R. (2000). *Naissance d'une Science Humaine: La Psychologie: Les Psychologues et le "Merveilleux Psychique."* Rennes: Presses Universitaires de Rennes.

Richet, C. (1922a). Mémoires et communications des membres et des correspondants de l'Académie: M. Charles Richet présente son livre: *Traité de Métapsychique* (Paris, Alcan, 1922; in-8°, 814 pages). *Compte Rendu Hebdomadaires des Séances de l'Académie des Sciences, 174,* 429–430.

Richet, C. (1922b). *Traité de Métapsychique.* Paris: Félix Alcan.

Richet, G., & Estingoy, P. (2003). Charles Richet et son temps. *Histoire des Sciences Médicales, 37,* 501–513.

Sudre, R. (1935). Charles Richet. *Journal de Débats Politiques et Littéraires,* December 5, 1.

Van Wijland, J. (Ed.). (2015). *Charles Richet (1850–1935): L'Exercice de la Curiosité.* Rennes: Presses Universitaires de Rennes.

Wolf, S. (1993). *Brain, Mind and Medicine: Charles Richet and the Origins of Physiological Psychology.* New Brunswick: Transaction Publishers.

Chapter 1

Aksakof, A., Schiaparelli, G., du Prel, C., Brofferio, A., Gerosa, G., Ermacora, G. B., & Finzi, G. (1893). Rapport de la commission réunie à Milan pour l'étude des phénomènes psychiques. *Annales des Sciences Psychiques, 3,* 39–64.

Alvarado, C.S. (2006). Human radiations: Concepts of force in mesmerism, spiritualism and psychical research. *Journal of the Society for Psychical Research, 70,* 138–162.

Alvarado, C.S. (2017). Telepathy, mediumship and psychology: Psychical research at the international congresses of psychology, 1889–1905. *Journal of Scientific Exploration, 31,* 255–292.

Alvarado, C.S., & Evrard, R. (2013). Nineteenth century psychical research in mainstream journals: The *Revue*

Philosophique de la France et de l'Étranger. Journal of Scientific Exploration, 27, 655–689.

Anonymous. (1905). Interviews on topics of the month: VI. On metapsychics: Professor Charles Richet. *Review of Reviews, 31,* 249–250.

Bourru, H., & Burot, P. (1886). Les premières expériences sur l'action des médicaments à distance. *Revue Philosophique de la France et de l'Étranger, 21,* 311–321.

Brower, M. B. (2010). *Unruly Spirits: The Science of Psychic Phenomena in Modern France.* Chicago: University of Illinois Press.

Bubb, E. M. (1936). Richet accepted survival before he died. *Psychic News* (30 May), 7.

Carroy, J. (2004). Playing with signatures: The young Charles Richet. In M.S. Micale (Ed.), *The Mind of Modernism: Medicine, Psychology, and the Cultural Arts in Europe and America, 1880–1940* (pp. 217–249). Stanford, CA: Stanford University Press.

de Vesme, C. (1919). L'enquête du Prof. Ch. Richet sur les faits métapsychiques aux armées. *Annales des Sciences Psychiques, 29,* 17–24.

Epheyre, C. (1889). Soeur Marthe. *Revue des Deux Mondes, 93,* 384–431.

Estingoy P. (2003). De la créativité chez le chercher: Un regard transversal sur l'oeuvre de Charles Richet. *Histoire des Sciences Médicales, 37,* 489–499.

Evrard, R. (2016). *Enquête sur 150 Ans de Parapsychologie: La Légende de l'Esprit.* Escalquens, France: Trajectoire.

Evrard, R., Gumpper, S., Beauvis, B., & Alvarado, C.S. (in press). "Never sacrifice anything to laboratory work": The "physiological psychology" of Charles Richet (1875-1905). *Journal of the History of the Behavioral Sciences.*

Flournoy, T. (1900). *From India to the Planet Mars: A Study of a Case of Somnabulism.* New York: Harper & Brothers.

Gauld, A. (1996). Notes on the career of the somnambule Léonie. *Journal of the Society for Psychical Research, 61,* 141–151.

Geley, G. (1921). Expériences de matérialisations avec M. Franek Kluski. *Bulletin de l'Institut Métapsychique International,* No. 4, 169–181.

Geley, G. (1927). *Clairvoyance and Materialisation.* London: Fisher Unwin. (Original work published in French, 1922)

Gurney, E., Myers, F.W.H., & and Podmore, F. (1886). *Phantasms of the Living* (2 vols.). London: Trübner.

Janet, P. (1886). Note sur quelques phénomènes de somnambulisme. *Revue Philosophique de la France et de l'Étranger, 21,* 190–198.

Janet, P. (1889). *L'Automatisme Psychologique.* Paris: Félix Alcan.

Lachapelle, S. (2011). *Investigating the Supernatural: From Spiritism and Occultism to Psychical Research and Metapsychics in France, 1853–1931.* Baltimore: Johns Hopkins University Press.

Leaf, W. (1890) A record of observations of certain phenomena of trance (3). Part II. *Proceedings of the Society for Psychical Research, 6,* 558–646.

Le Maléfan, P. (2002). Richet chasseur de fantômes: L'épisode de la villa Carmen. In B. Bensaude-Vincent & C. Blondel (Eds.), *Des Savants Face à l'Occulte 1870–1940* (pp. 173-200). Paris: La Découverte.

Lodge, O. J. (1894). Experience of unusual physical phenomena occurring in the presence of an entranced person (Eusapia Paladino). *Journal of the Society for Psychical Research, 6,* 306–336, 346–360.

Lodge, O. (1936). In memory of Charles Richet. *Proceedings of the Society for Psychical Research, 44,* 1–4.

Magalhães, S.N. (2007). *Charles Richet: O Apóstolo da Ciência e o Espiritismo.* São Paulo: FEB.

Monroe, J.W. (2008). *Laboratories of Faith: Mesmerism, Spiritism and Occultism in Modern France.* Ithaca: Cornell University Press.

Plas, R. (2000). *Naissance d'une Science Humaine: La Psychologie: Les Psychologues et le "Merveilleux Psychique."* Rennes: Presses Universitaires de Rennes.

Putnam, J.J. (1879). Richet on the physiology and histology of the cerebral convolutions. *Boston Medical and Surgical Journal, 101,* 815–816.

Richet, C. (1875). Du somnambulisme provoqué. *Journal de l'Anatomie et de la Physiologie Normales et Pathologiques de l'Homme et des Animaux, 11,* 348–378.

Richet, C. (1880). Les démoniaques d'aujourd'hui. *Revue des Deux Mondes, 50,* 340–372.

Richet, C. (1883). La personnalité et la memoire dans le somnambulisme. *Revue Philosophique de la France et de l'Étranger, 15,* 225–242.

Richet, C. (1884a). *L'Homme et l'Intelligence: Fragments de Physiologie et de Psychologie.* Paris: Félix Alcan.

Richet, C. (1884b). La suggestion mentale et le calcul des probabilités. *Revue Philosophique de la France et de l'Étranger, 18,* 609–674.

Richet, C. (1886a). L'action des substances toxiques et médicamenteuses a distance. *Revue Philosophique de la France et de l'Étranger, 21,* 321-323.

Richet, C. (1886b). Un fait de somnambulisme a distance. *Revue Philosophique de la France et de l'Étranger, 21,* 199-200.

Richet, C. (1886c). Les mouvements inconscients. In M. Berthelot (Ed.), *Hommage à Monsieur Chevreul a l'Occasion de Son Centenaire 31 Aout 1886* (pp. 79–84). Paris: Félix Alcan.

Richet, C. (1886d). De quelques phénomènes de suggestion sans hypnotism. *Revue Philosophique de la France et de l'Étranger, 21,* 324-326.

Richet, C. (1887). *Essai de Psychologie Générale.* Paris: Félix Alcan.

Richet, C. (1888a). Expériences sur le sommeil a distance. *Revue Philosophique de la France et de l'Étranger, 25,* 435–452.

Richet, C. (1888b). Relation de diverses expériences sur la transmission mentale, la lucidité, et autres phénomènes non explicables par les données scientifiques actuelles. *Proceedings of the Society for Psychical Research, 5,* 18–168.

Richet, C. (1889). Further experiments in hypnotic lucidity or clairvoyance. *Proceedings of the Society for Psychical Research, 6,* 66–83.

Richet, C. (1890). Les travaux du Congrès de Psychologie Physiologique. *Congrès International de Psychologie Physiologique* (pp. 32–38). Paris: Bureau de Revues.

Richet, C. (1891). Préface. In E. Gurney, F.W.H. Myers, & F. Podmore, *Les Hallucinations Télépathiques* (pp. v–xiii). Paris: Félix Alcan.

Richet, C. (1892). L'avenir de la psychologie. *International Congress of Experimental Psychology* (pp. 24–26). London: Williams & Norgate.

Richet, C. (1893). Expériences de Milan. *Annales des Sciences Psychiques, 3,* 1–31.

Richet, C. (1895). À propos des expériences faites avec Eusapia Paladino: Réponse à M. Hodgson. *Journal of the Society for Psychical Research 7,* 67–75.

Richet, C. (1899). *Les Guerres et la Paix.* Paris: C. Reinwald.

Richet, C. (1905a). Concerning the phenomenon called materialisation. *Annals of Psychical Science, 2,* 207–210, 269–289.

Richet, C. (1905b). La métapsychique. *Proceedings of the Society for Psychical Research, 19,* 2–49.

Richet, C. (1905c). Preface. In J. Maxwell, *Metapsychical Phenomena* (pp. xv–xxii). London: Duckworth. (Original work published, 1903)

Richet, C. (1906). The future of psychology. *Annals of Psychical Science, 4*, 201–216.

Richet, C. (1917). Avez-vous eu des pressentiments? *Bulletin des Armées de la République, 4*(266), 4.

Richet, C. (1919a). *Abregé d'Histoire Générale.* Paris: Hachette.

Richet, C. (1919b). *La Sélection Humaine.* Paris: Félix Alcan.

Richet, C. (1922). *Traité de Métapsychique.* Paris: Félix Alcan.

Richet, C. (1923a). Extra-sensorial channels of knowledge and the experimental method. *Lancet, 2*, 493–497.

Richet, C. (1923b). *Thirty Years of Psychical Research.* New York: Macmillan. (Translated from the second French edition of *Traité de métapsychique*)

Richet, C. (1924). Metapsychic science and survival. *Journal of the Society for Psychical Research, 21*, 274–278.

Richet, C. (1926). L'aviation triomphante. *Revue des Deux Mondes, 32*, 525–561.

Richet, C. (1932). Autobiographie. *Les Biographies Médicales, 6*, 145–160.

Richet, C. (1933a). *La Grande Espérance.* Paris: Montaigne.

Richet, C. (1933b). *Souvenirs d'un Physiologiste.* Paris: J. Peyronnet.

Richet, C. (1935). *Au Secours!* Paris: J. Peyronnet.

Richet, C. (n.d. a, ca 1931). *L'Avenir et la Prémonition.* Paris: Montaigne.

Richet, C. (n.d. b, ca 1929). *Our Sixth Sense.* London: Rider. (First published in French, 1928)

Richet, C., & Brund, R. (1903). *Circé.* Paris: Choudens.

Schneider W.H. (2001). Charles Richet and the social role of medical men. *Journal of Medical Biography, 9*, 213–219.

Schrenck-Notzing, Baron [A.] von. (1920). *Phenomena of Materialisation: A Contribution to the Investigation of*

Mediumistic Teleplastics (Rev. ed.). London: Paul Trench, Trubner.

Sidgwick, A., & Sidgwick, E.M. (1906). *Henry Sidgwick: A Memoir.* London: Macmillan.

Sudre, R. (1921). Einstein et la métapsychique: II. La physique des phénomènes supranormaux. *Revue Métapsychique.* No. 6, 307-316.

van Wijland, J. (ed.). (2015). *Charles Richet (1850–1935): L'Exercice de la Curiosité.* Rennes: Presses Universitaires de Rennes.

Wolf, S. (1993). *Brain, Mind and Medicine: Charles Richet and the Origins of Physiological Psychology.* New Brunswick: Transaction Publishers.

Chapter 2

Aksakof, A., Schiaparelli, G., du Prel, C., Brofferio, A., Gerosa, G., Ermacora, G. B., & Finzi, G. (1893). Rapport de la commission réunie à Milan pour l'étude des phénomènes psychiques. *Annales des Sciences Psychiques, 3,* 39–64.

Alvarado, C. S. (1993). Gifted subjects' contributions to psychical research: The case of Eusapia Palladino. *Journal of the Society for Psychical Research, 5,* 269–292.

Alvarado, C. S. (2011). Eusapia Palladino: An autobiographical essay. *Journal of Scientific Exploration, 25,* 77–101.

Alvarado, C.S. (2017). Telepathy, mediumship and psychology: Psychical research at the international congresses of psychology, 1889–1905. *Journal of Scientific Exploration, 31,* 255–292.

Alvarado, C. S., & Evrard, R. (2012). The psychic sciences in France: Historial notes on the *Annales des Sciences Psychiques. Journal of Scientific Exploration, 26,* 117–140.

Alvarado, C. S., & Evrard, R. (2013). Nineteenth century psychical research in mainstream journals: The *Revue Philosophique de la France et de l'Étranger*. *Journal of Scientific Exploration, 27,* 55–689.

Barrington, M. R., Stevenson, I., & Weaver, Z. (2005). *A World in a Grain of Sand: The Clairvoyance of Stefan Ossowiecki.* Jefferson, NC: McFarland.

Brower, M. B. (2010). *Unruly Spirits: The Science of Psychic Phenomena in Modern France.* Chicago: University of Illinois Press.

Carrington, H. (1909). *Eusapia Palladino and Her Phenomena.* New York: B.W. Dodge.

Carroy, J. (2004). Playing with signatures: The young Charles Richet. In M. S. Micale (Ed.), *The Mind of Modernism: Medicine, Psychology, and the Cultural Arts in Europe and America, 1880–1940* (pp. 217–249). Stanford, CA: Stanford University Press.

Carroy, J. (2015). Charles Richet au seuil du mystère. In J. van Wijland (Ed.), *Charles Richet (1850–1935): L'Exercice de la Curiosité* (pp. 65–79). Rennes: Presses Universitaires de Rennes.

Charcot, J.-M. (1882). Sur les divers états nerveux déterminés par l'hypnotisation chez les hystériques. *Comptes Rendus Hebdomadaires des Séances de l'Académie des Sciences, 94,* 403–405.

Dechambre, A. (1873). Mesmérisme. In A. Dehambre (Ed.), *Dictionnaire Encyclopédique des Sciences Médicales* (second series, Volume 7) (pp. 143–211). Paris: G. Masson.

Delanne, G. (1905). Les matérialisations de la Villa Carmen. *Revue Scientifique et Morale du Spiritisme, 11,* 257-268.

de Rochas, A. (1896). *L'Extériorisation de la Motricité: Recueil d'Expériences et d'Observations.* Paris: Chamuel.

Estingoy, P., & Ardiet, G. (2005). Du somnambulisme provoqué ... en 1875: Un préambule au développement scientifique de l'hypnose en France. *Annales Médico-Psychologiques, 163,* 344–350.

Evrard, R. (2016). *Enquête sur 150 Ans de Parapsychologie: La Légende de l'Esprit.* Escalquens, France: Trajectoire.

Gauld, A. (1968). *The Founders of Psychical Research.* London: Routledge & Kegan Paul.

Gauld, A. (1992). *A History of Hypnotism.* Cambridge: Cambridge University Press.

Geley, G. (1922). L'hypothèse spirite. *Revue Métapsychique,* No. 1, 20–33.

Gurney, E., Myers, F. W. H., & Podmore, F. (1886). *Phantasms of the Living* (2 volumes). London: Trübner.

Janet, P. (1886). Deuxième note sur le sommeil provoqué à distance et la suggestion mentale pendant l'état somnambulique. *Revue Philosophique de la France et de l'Étranger, 22,* 212–223.

Janet, P. (1923). À propos de la métapsychique. *Revue Philosophique de la France et de l'Étranger, 96,* 5–32.

Le Maléfan, P. (2002). Richet chasseur de fantômes: L'épisode de la villa Carmen. In B. Bansaude-Vincent & C. Blondel (Eds.), *Des Savants Face à l'Occulte 1870–1940* (pp. 173–200). Paris: La Découverte.

Lodge, O. J. (1894). Experience of unusual physical phenomena occurring in the presence of an entranced person (Eusapia Paladino). *Journal of the Society for Psychical Research, 34,* 306–336, 346–360.

Lodge, O. (1923). A textbook of metapsychics: Review and critique. *Proceedings of the Society for Psychical Research, 34,* 70–106.

Lodge, O. (1931). *Past Years: An Autobiography.* London: Hodder & Stoughton.

Nicolas, S. (2004). *L'Hypnose: Charcot Face à Bernheim: L'École de la Salpêtrière Face à L'École de Nancy.* Paris: L'Harmattan.

Nicolas, S., & Murray, D. J. (1999). Théodule Ribot (1839–1916), founder of French psychology: A biographical introduction. *History of Psychology, 2,* 277–301.

Ochorowicz, J. (1887). *De la Sugestion Mentale.* Paris: Octave Doin.

Piéron, H. (1922). Review of *Traité de Métapsychique* by C. Richet. *L'Anné Psychologique, 23,* 602–603.

Pierret, R. (1935). Review of *Souvenirs d'un Physiologiste* by C. Richet. *Journal de Physiologie et de Pathologie Générale, 33,* 1250.

Pilkington, R. (Ed.) (2013). *Men and Women of Parapsychology, Personal Reflections, Esprit, Volume 2.* San Antonio, TX: Anomalist Books.

Plas, R. (2000). *Naissance d'une Science Humaine: La Psychologie: Les Psychologues et le "Merveilleux Psychique."* Rennes: Presses Universitaires de Rennes.

Rhine, L. E. (1983). *Something Hidden.* Jefferson, NC: McFarland.

Richet, C. (1875). Du somnambulisme provoqué. *Journal de l'Anatomie et de la Physiologie Normales et Pathologiques de l'Homme et des Animaux, 11,* 348–378.

Richet, C. (1883). La personnalité et la memoire dans le somnambulisme. *Revue Philosophique de la France et de l'Étranger, 15,* 225–242.

Richet, C. (1884a). *L'Homme et l'Intelligence: Fragments de Physiologie et de Psychologie.* Paris: Félix Alcan.

Richet, C. (1884b). La suggestion mentale et le calcul des probabilités. *Revue Philosophique de la France et de l'Étranger, 18,* 609–674.

Richet, C. (1886). Un fait de somnambulisme à distance. *Revue Philosophique de la France et de l'Étranger, 21,* 199–200.

Richet, C. (1888). Relation de diverses expériences sur la transmission mentale, la lucidité, et autres phénomènes non explicables par les données scientifiques actuelles. *Proceedings of the Society for Psychical Research, 5*, 18–168.

Richet, C. (1889). Further experiments in hypnotic lucidity or clairvoyance. *Proceedings of the Society for Psychical Research, 6*, 66–83.

Richet, C. (1891). Des phénomènes psychiques: Lettre à M. Dariex. *Annales des Sciences Psychiques, 1*, 1-8.

Richet, C. (1893a). Expériences de Milan. *Annales des Sciences Psychiques, 3*, 1–31.

Richet, C. (1893b). Le hasard et la probabilité: Note relative aux expériences de M. Roux. *Annales des Sciences Psychiques, 3*, 209–211.

Richet, C. (1894). *Exposé des Travaux Scientifiques de M. Charles Richet.* Paris: Chamerot and Renouard.

Richet, C. (1895). À propos des expériences faites avec Eusapia Paladino: Réponse à M. Hodgson. *Journal of the Society for Psychical Research 7*, 67–75.

Richet, C. (1899). On the conditions of certainty. *Proceedings of the Society for Psychical Research, 14*, 152–157.

Richet, C. (1901). In memoriam Frederic W. H. Myers. *Annales des Sciences Psychiques, 11*, 173–178.

Richet, C. (1905a). Concerning the phenomenon called materialisation. *Annals of Psychical Science, 2*, 207–210, 269–289.

Richet, C. (1905b). La métapsychique. *Proceedings of the Society for Psychical Research, 19*, 2–49.

Richet, C. (1907). "Metapsychism" or "occultism"? *Annals of Psychical Science, 6*, 423–425.

Richet, C. (1922). *Traité de Métapsychique.* Paris: Félix Alcan.

Richet, C. (1923). *Thirty Years of Psychical Research.* New York: Macmillan.

Richet, C. (1924). Metapsychic science and survival. *Journal of the Society for Psychical Research, 21*, 274–278.

Richet, C. (1925). La science métapsychique. *La Presse Médicale, 33,* 857–862.

Richet, C. (1933). *Souvenirs d'un Physiologiste.* Paris: J. Peyronnet.

Richet, C. (n.d. ca 1928). *Our Sixth Sense.* London: Rider. [First published in French 1928]

Ruault, A. (1886). Le mécanisme de la suggestion mentale hypnotique. *Revue Philosophique de la France et de l'Étranger, 22,* 679–697.

Venzano, G. (1906). Some phenomena of transmission of thought, in relation to mediumship. *Annals of Psychical Science, 3,* 17–46.

Wolf, S. (1993). *Brain, Mind and Medicine: Charles Richet and the Origins of Physiological Psychology.* New Brunswick: Transaction Publishers.

Chapter 3

Alvarado, C. S. (2006). Human radiations: Concepts of force in mesmerism, spiritualism and psychical research. *Journal of the Society for Psychical Research, 70,* 138–162.

Alvarado, C.S. (2015). Telepathic emissions: Edwin J. Houston on "Cerebral Radiation." *Journal of Scientific Exploration, 29,* 467–490.

Alvarado, C.S., & Evrard, R. (2013). Nineteenth century psychical research in mainstream journals: The *Revue Philosophique de la France et de l'Étranger. Journal of Scientific Exploration, 27,* 655-689.

Barrett, W. F., Gurney, E., & Myers, F. W. H. (1882). First report on thought-reading. *Proceedings of the Society for Psychical Research, 1,* 13–34.

Barrett, W. F., Massey, C. C., Moses, W. S., Podmore, F., Gurney, E., & Myers, F. W. H. (1884). Third report of the Literary Committee: A theory of apparitions: Part I. *Proceedings of the Society for Psychical Research, 2*, 109–136.

Beaunis, H. (1886). Un fait de suggestion mentale. *Revue Philosophique de la France et de l'Étranger, 21*, 204.

Carroy, J. (2004). Playing with signatures: The young Charles Richet. In M.S. Micale (Ed.), *The Mind of Modernism: Medicine, Psychology, and the Cultural Arts in Europe and America, 1880–1940* (pp. 217–249). Stanford University Press.

Chevreul, M. E. (1854). *De la Baguette Divinatoire, du Pendule dit Explorateur et des Tables Tournantes.* Paris: Mallet-Bachelier.

Dufay, Dr. (1888). Contribution à l'étude du somnambulisme provoqué à distance et à l'insu du sujet. *Revue Philosophique de la France et de l'Étranger, 26*, 301–312.

Franklin, C. L. (1885). Richet on mental suggestion. *Science, 5*, 132–134.

Gurney, E. (1884). M. Richet's recent researches in thought-transference. *Proceedings of the Society for Psychical Research, 2*, 239–264.

Hacking, I. (1988). Telepathy: Origins of randomization in experimental design. *Isis, 79*, 427–451.

Jahn, R. G., & Dunne, B. J. (1987). *Margins of Reality: The Role of Consciousness in the Physical World.* Harcourt Brace Jovanovich.

Janet, P. (1886a). Note sur quelques phénomènes de sonambulisme. *Revue Philosophique de la France et de l'Étranger, 21*, 190–198.

Janet, P. (1886b). Deuxième note sur le somneil provoqué a distance et la suggestion mentale pendant l'état somnambulique. *Revue Philosophique de la France et de l'Étranger, 22*, 212–223.

Myers, F. W. H. (1884). On a telepathic explanation of some so-called spiritualistic phenomena: Part I. *Proceedings of the Society for Psychical Research, 2*, 217–237.

Myers, F. W. H. (1885). Automatic writing. – II. *Proceedings of the Society for Psychical Research, 3,* 1–63.

Ochorowicz, J. (1887). *De la Suggestion Mentale.* Paris: Octave Doin.

Plas, R. (2000). *Naissance d'une Science Humaine: La Psychologie: Les Psychologues et le "Merveilleux Psychique."* Presses Universitaires de Rennes.

Rhine, J. B. (1947). *The Reach of the Mind.* New York: William Sloane.

Richet, C. (1884). La suggestion mentale et le calcul des probabilités. *Revue Philosophique de la France et de l'Étranger, 18,* 609–674.

Richet, C. (1886). Les mouvements inconscients. In M. Berthelot (Ed.), *Hommage à Monsieur Chevreul a l'Occasion de son Centenaire 31 Aout 1886* (pp. 79–84). Paris: Félix Alcan.

Richet, C. (1888). Relation de diverses expériences sur la transmission mentale, la lucidité, et autres phénomènes non explicables par les données scientifiques actuelles. *Proceedings of the Society for Psychical Research, 5,* 18–168.

Richet, C. (1889). Further experiments in hypnotic lucidity or clairvoyance. *Proceedings of the Society for Psychical Research, 6,* 66–83.

Richet, C. (n.d.). *Our Sixth Sense.* London: Rider.

Rogers, E. C. (1853). *Philosophy of Mysterious Agents, Human and Mundane; or, the Dynamic Laws and Relations of Man.* Boston: John P. Jewett.

Chapter 4

Alvarado, C.S. (2006). Aspects of the history of parapsychology: I. Psychical Research at the 1889 International Congress of Physiological Psychology. Retrieved from http://www.pflyceum.org/162.html

Alvarado, C.S. (2009). Psychical research in the *Psychological Review*, 1894–1900: A bibliographical note. *Journal of Scientific Exploration, 23*, 211–220.

Alvarado, C.S. (2014). G. Stanley Hall on "Mystic or Borderline Phenomena." *Journal of Scientific Exploration, 28*, 75–93.

Alvarado, C.S. (2017). Telepathy, mediumship, and psychology: Psychical research at the International Congresses of Psychology, 1889–1905. *Journal of Scientific Exploration, 31*, 54-101.

Carrington, H. (1915). "Freudian psychology and psychical research" (A rejoinder). *Journal of Abnormal Psychology, 9*, 411–416.

Carroy, J., & Schmidgen, H. (2006). Psychologies expérimentales: Leipzig-Paris-Würzburg (1890–1910). *Milf Neuf Cent, 24*, 171–204.

Coon, D. J. (1992). Testing the limits of sense and science: American experimental psychologists combat spiritualism, 1880-1920. *American Psychologist, 47*, 143–151.

De Sanctis, S. (Ed.). (1906). *Atti del V Congresso Internazionale di Psicologia*. Rome: Forzani.

Estingoy, P., & Ardiet, G. (2005). Du somnambulisme provoqué … en 1875: Un préambule au développement scientifique de l'hypnose en France. *Annales Médico-Psychologiques, 163*, 344–350.

Evrard, R., Pratte, E.A., & Cardeña, E. (2018). Pierre Janet and the enchanted boundary of psychical research. *History of Psychology, 21*, 100–125.

Gurney, E., Myers, F.W.H., & Podmore, F. (1886). *Phantasms of the Living* (2 vols.). London: Trübner.

[Hall, G. S.]. (1887). [Review of Proceedings *of the Society for Psychical Research*, and *Phantasms of the Living*, by E. Gurney, F.W.H. Myers, and F. Podmore.] *American Journal of Psychology, 1*, 128–146.

Hansen, F. C. C., & Lehmann, A. (1895). Ueber unwillkürliches Flüstern, eine kritische und experimentelle Untersuchung der sogenannten Gedakenübertragung. *Philosophische Studien, 11,* 471–530.

James, W. (1896). Psychical research. *Psychological Review, 3,* 649–652.

Janet, P. (Ed.). (1901). *IVe Congrès International de Psychologie.* Paris: Félix Alcan.

Jastrow, J. (1889). The problems of "psychic research." *Harper's New Monthly Magazine, 79,* 76–82.

Le Maléfan, P. (1995). Sciences psychiques, métapsychiques et psychologie: Côtoiement et divorce: Histoire d'un partage. *Bulletin de Psychologie, 48,* 624–630.

Marshall, M. E., & Went, R. A. (1980). Wilhelm Wundt, spiritism, and the assumptions of science. In W. G. Bringmann & R.D. Tweney (Eds.), *Wundt Studies: A Centennial Collection* (pp. 158–175). Toronto: C. J. Hogrefe.

Maxwell, J. (1907). Psychologie et métapsychique. *L'Année Psychologique, 13,* 100–113.

Moser, F. (1935). *Der Okkultismus: Täuschungen und Tatsachen* (2 vols.) Munich: Ernst Reinhard.

Nicolas, S., & Meunier, F. (2002). The causes, course and consequences of the first international psychology congress stand in Paris in 1889. *Theorie & Modelli, 7,* 19–40.

Piéron, H. (1954). Histoire succinte des congrés internationaux de psychologie. *L'Année Psychologique, 2,* 397–405.

Richet, C. (1875). Du somnambulisme provoqué. *Journal de l'Anatomie et de la Physiologie Normales et Pathologiques de l'Homme et des Animaux, 11,* 348–378.

Richet, C. (1890). Les travaux du Congrès de psychologie physiologique. *Congrès International de Psychologie Physiologique* (pp. 32–38). Paris: Bureau de Revues.

Richet, C. (1892). L'avenir de la psychologie. *International Congress of Experimental Psychology* (pp. 24–26). London: Williams & Norgate.

Richet, C. (1905a). Concerning the phenomenon called materialisation. *Annals of Psychical Science, 2,* 207–210, 269–289.

Richet, C. (1905b). La métapsychique. *Proceedings of the Society for Psychical Research, 19,* 2–49.

Richet, C. (1905c). Xenoglossie: L'écriture automatique en langues étrangères. *Proceedings of the Society for Psychical Research, 19,* 162–194.

Richet, C. (1906a). L'avenir de la psychologie. In S. De Sanctis (Ed.), *Atti del V Congresso Internazionale di Psicologia* (pp. 166–173). Rome: Forzani.

Richet, C. (1906b). The future of psychology. *Annals of Psychical Science, 4,* 201–216.

Richet, C. (1922). *Traité de Métapsychique.* Paris: Félix Alcan.

Richet, C. (1933a). *La Grande Espérance.* Paris: Montaigne.

Richet, C. (1933b). *Souvenirs d'un Physiologiste.* Paris: J. Peyronnet.

Richet, C. (1935). *Au Secours!* Paris: J. Peyronnet.

Sava, G. (2010). Line storiche dei primi congressi internazionali di psicologia (dal 1889 al 1905). In G. Ceccarelli (Ed.), *La Psicologia Italiana all'inizio del Novecento* (pp. 49-63). Milan: FrancoAngeli.

Sidgwick, A., & Sidgwick, E.M. (1906). *Henry Sidgwick: A Memoir.* London: Macmillan.

Sidgwick, H. (1892). Statistical inquiry into hallucinations. *International Congress of Experimental Psychology* (pp. 56–61). London: Williams & Norgate.

Sidgwick, H., Johnson, A., Myers, F.W.H., Podmore, F., & Sidgwick, E.M. (1894). Report on the Census of Hallucinations. *Proceedings of the Society for Psychical Research, 10,* 25–422.

Sommer, A. (2012). Psychical research and the origins of American psychology: Hugo Münsterberg, William James, and Eusapia Palladino. *History of the Human Sciences, 25,* 23–44.

Sommer, A. (2013). *Crossing the Boundaries of Mind and Body: Psychical Research and the Origins of Modern Psychology.* PhD thesis, University College of London.

Statistique des Hallucinations. (1890). *Congrès International de Psychologie Physiologique* (pp. 151–157). Paris: Bureau de Revues.

Sudre, R. (1926). *Introduction à la Métapsychique Humaine.* Paris: Payot.

Taves, A. (2014). A tale of two congresses: The psychological study of psychical, occult, and religious phenomena, 1900–1909. *Journal of the History of the Behavioral Sciences, 50,* 376–399.

Troland, L. T. (1914). The Freudian psychology and psychical research. *Journal of Abnormal Psychology, 8,* 405–428.

Wundt, W. (2000). *Hipnotismo y Sugestión.* Jaén, Spain: Del Lunar. (Original work published 1892)

Chapter 5

Alvarado, C. S. (2006). Human radiations: Concepts of force in mesmerism, spiritualism and psychical research. *Journal of the Society for Psychical Research, 70,* 138–162.

Alvarado, C.S. (2016). Richet's Traité de Métapsychique (Thirty Years of Psychical Research). In R. McLuhan (Ed.), *Psi Encyclopedia.* London: Society for Psychical Research. Retrieved from http://psi-encyclopedia.spr.ac.uk/book-reviews/richets-traite-de-metapsychique-thirty-years-of-psychical-research

Alvarado, C.S. (2017). Telepathy, mediumship and psychology: Psychical research at the international congresses of psychology, 1889–1905. *Journal of Scientific Exploration, 31*, 255–292.

Anonymous. (1922a). Les mystéres du spiritisme: Les premiers resultats du concours métapsychique du "Matin." *Le Matin*, August 3, 1.

Anonymous. (1922b). Review of *Traité de Métapsychique*, by C. Richet. *Revue Bibliographique, 3*, 639–640.

Anonymous. (1922c). A travers les livres. *Le Petit Parisien*, February 28, 5.

Bénézech, A. (1922). "Traité de Métapsychique." *Revue Spirite, 65*, 170–177.

Blier, J. (1922). A la dérive: A propos du livre de M. Charles Richet sur la métapsychique. *Revue de Pathologie Comparée et d'Hygiene Générale, 22*, 253–259.

Bourget, P. (1922). Du métapsychisme. *L'Illustration, 80*, 65–66.

Bozzano, E. (1922). Considerazioni intorno al "Traité de Métapsychique" del Prof. Charles Richet. *Luce e Ombra, 22*, 103–115.

Bricout, J. (1923). La "métapsychique" du Professeur Richet. *L'Ouest-Éclair*, November 15, 1.

Brower, M.B. (2010). *Unruly Spirits: The Science of Psychic Phenomena in Modern France.* Urbana, IL: University of Illinois Press.

Carrington, H. (1908). *The Coming Science.* Boston: Small, Maynard.

Ceccarelli, L. (2001). *Shaping Science with Rhetoric: The Case of Dobzhansky, Schrödinger, and Wilson.* Chicago: University of Chicago Press.

Challaye, F. (1920-1922). Traité de Métapsychique. In C. Auge (ed.), *Larousse Mensuel Illustré* (Vol. 5, p. 987). Paris: Librairie Larousse.

Chassaigne, L. (1922). Une science nouvelle: La métapsychique. *Le Journal*, July 12, 4.

Coon, D. J. (1992). Testing the limits of sense and science: American experimental psychologists combat spiritualism, 1880–1920. *American Psychologist, 47*, 143–151.

Coste, A. (1895). *Les Phénomènes Psychiques Occultes: État Actual de la Question.* Montpellier: Camille Coulet.

Curnow, L. (1923). Richet and Spiritualism. *Light, 43*, 580.

de Fleury, M. (1922). Essai sur la crédulité. *Le Figaro*, August 1, 1.

Deleuze, J.P.F. (1813). *Histoire Critique du Magnétisme Animal* (2 vols). Paris: Mame.

de Rochas, A. (1899). *L'Extériorisation de la Sensibilité: Étude Expérimentale & Historique* (5th ed.) Paris: Chamuel.

de Varigny, H. (1922). La métapsychique et la cryptesthésie. *Journal de Débats Politiques et Littéraires, 29*, 394–395.

Driesch, H. (1924). Reviews of *Metapsichica Moderna*, by W. Mackenzie, and *Grundiss der Parapsychologie und der Parapsychophysik*, by C. Richet. *Psychische Studien, 51*, 34–49.

Evrard, R. (2016). *La Légende de l'Esprit: Enquête sur 150 Ans de Parapsychologie.* Paris: Trajectoire.

F., R. (1922). Revue des livres. *Bibliothèque Universelle et Revue Suisse, 127*, iii-xxiii.

Ferrand, J. (1922). Sciences occultes et médicales. Biologie et hygiene. *Polybiblion: Revue Bibliographique Universelle, 155*(s.2) 81–95.

Ferrari, G. (1922). Review of *Traité de Métapsychique*, by C. Richet. *Rivista di Psicologia, 18*, 45.

Flammarion, C. (1920–1922). *La Mort et son Mystère.* (3 vols.) Paris: Ernest Flammarion.

Geley, G. (1919). La science du mystère s'organise. *Le Journal*, November 10, 1–2.

Geley, G. (1921). Expériences de matérialisations avec M. Franek Kluski. *Bulletin de l'Institut Métapsychique International*, No. 3, 117–126.

Geley, G. (1922). L'hypothèse spirite. *Revue Métapsychique*, No. 1, 120–133.

Geley, G. (1927). *Clairvoyance and Materialisation.* London: T. Fisher Unwin (First published in French, 1924).

Gieryn, T. F. (1999). *Cultural Boundaries of Science: Credibility on the Line.* Chicago: University of Chicago Press.

Guitet-Vauquelin, P. (1922). Les morts vivent-ils? *Revue de la Semaine Illustrée*, 3, 471–490.

Gutierez, G., & Maillard, N. (2005). *Les Aventuriers de l'Esprit.* Paris: Presses du Châtelet.

[Hall, G. S.] (1887). Review of *Proceedings of the Society for Psychical Research*, and *Phantasms of the Living*, by E. Gurney, F. W. H. Myers, and F. Podmore. *American Journal of Psychology*, 1, 128–146.

Hartenberg, P. (1924). Review of *Traité de Métapsychique*, by C. Richet. *Le Presse Médicale*, No. 16, 323–324.

Heuzé, P. (1921a). Les morts vivent-ils? Enquête sur l'état present des sciences psychiques. *L'Opinion*, September 3, 262–265.

Heuzé, P. (1921b). *Les Morts Vivent-Ils? Enquête sur l'État Présent des Sciences Psychiques.* Paris: Renaissance du livre.

Heuzé, P. (1922a). Les morts vivent-ils? IV Les médiums.— Eva. *L'Opinion*, August 4, 12–36.

Heuzé, P. (1922b). Les morts vivent-ils? X Le rapport. *L'Opinion*, September 15, 771–791.

Heuzé, P.(1922c). *Les Morts Vivent-Ils ? 2e série. L'Ectoplasme.* Paris: La Renaissance du Livre.

Holt, H. (1922). A review of Richet. *Journal of the American Society for Psychical Research*, 16, 655–670.

Janet, P. (1923). A propos de la métapsychique. *Revue Philosophique de la France et de l'Étranger*, 96, 5–32.

Jastrow, J. (1889). The problems of "psychic research." *Harper's New Monthly Magazine, 79*, 76–82.

Lapicque, L. Dumas, G., Piéron, H., & Laugier, H. (1922). Rapport sur des expériences de contrôle relatives aux phénomènes dits ectoplasmiques. *L'Année Psychologique, 23*, 604–611.

Latour, B. (1922). La métapsychique et les phénomènes "ectoplasmiques." *La Croix*, July 26, 3.

Levy-Valensi, J. (1922). Au sujet du Traité de Métapsychique du Professeur Richet. *L'Encéphale, 17*, 297–304.

Lodge, O. (1923). A textbook of metapsychics: Review and critique. *Proceedings of the Society for Psychical Research, 34*, 70–106.

Marmin, N. (2001). Métapsychique et psychologie en France (1880–1940). *Revue d'Histoire des Sciences Humaines, 4*, 145–171.

N, R. (1922). Review of *Traité de Métapsychique*, by C. Richet. *Journal de l'Association Médicale Mutualle, 25*, 183–184.

Nordmann, C. (1922). Pour aborder la métapsychique. *Revue des Deux Mondes, 92*(s.7), 935–946.

Olivier, P. (1922). Esotérisme et sciences psychiques. *Mercure de France, 33*, 484–492.

Osty, E. (1923). *Supernormal Faculties in Man.* London: Methuen. (First published in 1923)

Piéron, H. (1922). Review of *Traité de Métapsychique*, by C. Richet. *L'Année Psychologique, 23*, 602–603.

Podmore, F. (1897). *Studies in Psychical Research.* London: K. Paul, Trench, Trubner.

Putnam, J. J. (1879). Richet on the physiology and histology of the cerebral convolutions. *Boston Medical and Surgical Journal, 101*, 815–816.

Reichenbach, C. von. (1851). *Physico-Physiological Researches on the Dynamics of Magnetism, Electricity, Heat, Light,*

Crystallization, and Chemism, in their Relation to Vital Force (from German 2nd ed). New York: J.S. Redfield (First published in German, 1849)

Richet, C. (1899). Les promesses de la science. *Revue Scientifique, 11*(3), 33–35.

Richet, C. (1905). La métapsychique. *Proceedings of the Society for Psychical Research, 19*, 2–49.

Richet, C. (1922a). Mémoires et communications des membres et des correspondants de l'Académie: M. Charles Richet présente son livre: *Traité de Métapsychique* (Paris, Alcan, 1922; in-8°, 814 pages). *Compte Rendu Hebdomadaires des Séances de l'Académie des Sciences, 174*, 429–430.

Richet, C. (1922b). *Traité de Métapsychique.* Paris: Félix Alcan.

Richet, C. (1923a). *Grundiss der Parapsychologie und der Parapsychophysik.* Stuttgart: Deutsche Verlagsges.

Richet, C. (1923b). *Thirty Years of Psychical Research.* New York: Macmillan.

Richet, C. (1923c). *Tratado de Metapsíquica.* Barcelona: Araluce.

Richet, C. (1924). For and against survival: The difficulty of survival from the scientific point of view. *Proceedings of the Society for Psychical Research, 34*, 107–113.

Richet, C. (1933). *Souvenirs d'un Physiologiste.* Paris: J. Peyronnet.

Sommer, A. (2013). *Crossing the Boundaries of Mind and Body: Psychical Research and the Origins of Modern Psychology.* Ph.D. thesis, University College of London.

Stephens, F. (1923). Professor Richet and psychical research: The question of brain and mind. *Light, 43*, 546-547.

Sudre, R. (1922). Review of *Traité de Métapsychique*, by C. Richet. *Revue Métapsychique*, No. 2, 144–148.

Wolf, S. (1993). *Brain, Mind and Medicine: Charles Richet and the Origins of Physiological Psychology.* New Brunswick: Transaction Publishers.

Chapter 6

Aksakof, A. (1875). Researches on the historical origin of the reincarnation speculations of French Spiritualists. *Spiritual Newspaper*, August 13, 74–75.

Alvarado, C.S. (2010). Classic text No. 84: 'Divisions of personality and spiritism' by Alfred Binet (1896). *History of Psychiatry*, 21, 487–500.

Alvarado CS (2011). On mediumistic personation phenomena [Letter to the editor]. *Journal of the Society for Psychical Research* 75, 59–61.

Alvarado, C.S. (2014). Mediumship, psychical research, dissociation, and the powers of the subconscious mind. *Journal of Parapsychology, 78*, 98–114.

Alvarado, C.S. (2016). Classic Text No. 107: Joseph Maxwell on mediumistic personifications. *History of Psychiatry, 27*, 350–366.

Alvarado, C.S., Maraldi, E. de O., Machado, F.R., & Zangari, W. (2014). Théodore Flournoy's contributions to psychical research. *Journal of the Society for Psychical Research, 78*, 149–168.

Alvarado, C.S., Nahm, M., & Sommer, A. (2012). Notes on early interpretations of mediumship. *Journal of Scientific Exploration, 26*, 855–865.

Alvarado, C.S., & Zingrone, N.L. (2012). Classic Text No. 90: 'The Pathology and Treatment of Mediomania', by Frederic Rowland Marvin (1874). *History of Psychiatry, 23*, 229–244.

Alvarado, C.S., & Zingrone, N.L. (2015). Note on the reception of Théodore Flournoy's *Des Indes à la Planète Mars. Journal of the Society for Psychical Research, 79*, 156–164.

Carpenter, W.B. (1877). *Mesmerism and Spiritualism, &c.: Historically and Scientifically Considered*. London: Longmans and Green.

Carroy, J. (1993). *Les Personnalités Doubles et Multiples: Entre Science et Fiction*. Paris: Presses Universitaires de France.

Crabtree, A. (1993). *From Mesmer to Freud: Magnetic Sleep and the Roots of Psychological Healing*. New Haven, CT: Yale University Press.

Flammarion, C. (1907). *Mysterious Psychic Forces*. Boston: Small, Maynard.

Flournoy, T. (1900). *From India to the Planet Mars: A Study of a Case of Somnabulism*. New York: Harper & Brothers.

Flournoy, T. (1911). *Spiritism and Psychology*. New York: Harper and Brothers.

Hammond, W.A. (1876). *Spiritualism and Allied Causes and Conditions of Nervous Derangement*. New York: G.P. Putnam's.

Hart, J.A. (1913). *Sardou and the Sardou Plays*. Philadelphia: J.B. Lippincott.

Hyslop, J.H. (1906). *Borderland of Psychical Research*. Boston: Herbert B. Turner.

Janet, P. (1889). *L'Automatisme Psychologique*. Paris: Félix Alcan.

Le Maléfan, P. (1999). *Folie et Spiritisme: Histoire du Discourse Psychopathologique sur la Pratique du Spiritisme, ses Abords et ses Avatars (1850–1950)*. Paris: L'Hartmattan.

Maraldi, E. de O., & Alvarado, C.S. (2018). Classic Text No. 113: Final chapter, From India to the Planet Mars: A Study of a Case of Somnambulism with Glossolalia, by Théodore Flournoy (1900). *History of Psychiatry, 29*, 110–125.

Maxwell, J. (1905) *Metapsychical Phenomena: Methods and Observations*. London: Duckworth. (First published in French 1903)

Myers, F.W.H. (1884). On a telepathic explanation of some so-called spiritualistic phenomena: Part I. *Proceedings of the Society for Psychical Research, 2*, 217–237.

Myers, F.W.H. (1903). *Human Personality and its Survival of Bodily Death* (2 vols.). London: Longmans, Green.

Richet, C. (1883). La personnalité et la memoire dans le somnambulisme. *Revue Philosophique de la France et de l'Étranger, 15*, 225–242.

Richet, C. (1884). La suggestion mentale et le calcul des probabilités. *Revue Philosophique de la France et de l'Étranger, 18*, 609–674.

Richet, C. (1888). Relation de diverses expériences sur la transmission mentale, la lucidité, et autres phénomènes non explicables par les données scientifiques actuelles. *Proceedings of the Society for Psychical Research, 5*, 18–168.

Richet, C. (1889). Further experiments in hypnotic lucidity or clairvoyance. *Proceedings of the Society for Psychical Research, 6*, 66–83.

Richet, C. (1905). La métapsychique. *Proceedings of the Society for Psychical Research, 19*, 2–49.

Richet, C. (1923). *Thirty Years of Psychical Research.* New York: Macmillan.

Rogers, E. C. (1853). *Philosophy of Mysterious Agents, Human and Mundane; Or, the Dynamic Laws and Relations of Man.* Boston: J. P. Jewett.

Sardou, V. (1858). Des habitations de la planète Jupiter. *Revue Spirite: Journal d'Études Psychologiques, 1*, 223–232.

Shamdasani, S. (1994). Encountering Hélène: Théodore Flournoy and the genesis of subliminal psychology. In T. Flournoy, *From India to the Planet Mars* (pp. xi–li). Princeton, NJ: Princeton University Press.

Sudre, R. (1926). *Introduction à la Métapsychique Humaine.* Paris: Payot.

Sudre, R. (1946). *Personnages d'Au-Delà.* Paris: Société des Éditions de Noël.

Appendix A

Hodgson, R. (1892). A record of observations of certain phenomena of trance. *Proceedings of the Society for Psychical Research, 8*, 1–167.

Hodgson, R. (1898). A further record of observations of certain phenomena of trance. *Proceedings of the Society for Psychical Research, 13*, 284–582.

Hyslop, J.H. (1901). A further record of observations of certain phenomena of trance. *Proceedings of the Society for Psychical Research, 16*, 1–649.

James, W. (1886). Report of the Committee on Mediumistic Phenomena. *Proceedings of the American Society for Psychical Research, 1*, 102–106.

James, W. (1890). A record of observations of certain phenomena of trance: Part III. *Proceedings of the Society for Psychical Research, 6*, 651–659.

Leaf, W. (1890). A record of observations of certain phenomena of trance (3). Part II. *Proceedings of the Society for Psychical Research, 6*, 558–646.

Lodge, O. (1890a). A record of observations of certain phenomena of trance (2). Part I. *Proceedings of the Society for Psychical Research, 6*, 443–557.

Lodge, O. (1890b). Index to items in Parts I. and II. specially difficult to explain by direct Thought-transference: i.e., by any agency exerted by the sitter. *Proceedings of the Society for Psychical Research, 6*, 647–650.

Myers, F. W. H. (1890). A record of observations of certain phenomena of trance (1). Introduction. *Proceedings of the Society for Psychical Research, 6*, 436–442.

Newbold, W.R. (1898) A further record of observations of certain phenomena of trance. *Proceedings of the Society for Psychical Research, 14*, 6–49.

Richet, C. (1905). La métapsychique. *Proceedings of the Society for Psychical Research, 19,* 2–49.

Richet, C. (1922) *Traité de Métapsychique.* Paris: Félix Alcan.

Appendix C

Demarest, M. (2013). Spirits of the trade: Teleplasm, ectoplasm, psychoplasm, ideoplasm. *Psypioneer Journal, 9,* 88–98. Retrieved from http://www.iapsop.com/psypioneer/psypioneer_v9_n3_mar_2013.pdf

Granger, M. (2014). D'où vient le mot "ectoplasme" dans son acception spirite et métapsychique? *Revue Spirite, 157*(2), 15–17.

Lodge, O. J. (1894). Experience of unusual physical phenomena occurring in the presence of an entranced person (Eusapia Paladino). *Journal of the Society for Psychical Research, 6,* 306–336, 346–360.

Richet, C. (1895). À propos des expériences faites avec Eusapia Paladino: Réponse à M. Hodgson. *Journal of the Society for Psychical Research 7,* 67–75.

Richet, C. (1922). *Traité de Métapsychique.* Paris: Félix Alcan.

Notes

～

Chapter 1

[1] For more information about these early years see Chapter 2 of the current work.

[2] For a discussion of Leboulanger see Gauld (1996). Plas (2000) has discussed her double role as a producer of dissociative and parapsychological phenomena in her work with Janet and Richet.

[3] On speculations about Einstein's ideas and physical mediumship see Sudre (1921).

Chapter 2

[1] Richet stated before that there are occult phenomena but in the sense of being unknown (Richet, 1891, p. 2). In other publications he rejected the term occultism (Richet, 1907, p. 423, 1922, p. 2).

[2]   Regarding his ability to hypnotize, Richet (1922, p. 121)
       wrote years earlier that he used to induce trance with ease
       in the old days but that at present it was the opposite. He
       also pointed out that he had heard the same from other
       hypnotizers.

[3]   One of the oldest hospitals in Paris.

[4]   French physician Henri Liouville (1837–1887), who taught
       at the Faculté de Médicine, Paris.

[5]   This probably is French surgeon Léon Clément Le Fort
       (1829–1893). See Richet's (1886) report of the tests with
       the woman, a patient of about 25 years of age.

[6]   This was French physician Amédée Dechambre (1812–
       1886). In his article he concluded that because the effects
       in question were produced by "a cause other than a
       special agent called magnetism, we conclude with this
       radical conclusion: ANIMAL MAGNETISM DOES NOT
       EXIST" (Dechambre, 1873, p. 207). What Dechambre
       opposed was the explanation of phenomena via the
       concept of the force referred to as animal magnetism.
       He believed that an overexcited imagination, affected
       as well by the social contagion involved in rituals, could
       have "repercussions on the nervous system, and … on
       organic actions," enhancing or diminishing sensibility,
       and "exerting a real action on the course of disease"
       (Dechambre, 1873, p. 206). As for Richet, he did not say
       what he believed, but we know from his writings (e.g.,
       Richet, 1884a) that he did not believe in a magnetic
       force. I have not found evidence that he interpreted his
       difficulties to use hypnosis in later years as evidence for
       the existence of such a force. In later years Richet (1922,
       pp. 121–122) expressed doubts about magnetism, pointing
       out the difficulty in controlling for suggestion.

[7]   Richet's first sentence in the paper was: "It takes some
       courage to utter aloud the word somnambulism" (Richet,
       1875, p. 348). This paper has been considered very
       important in the history of French hypnosis (e.g., Estingoy

& Ardiet, 2005). Charles-Philippe Robin (1821–1885) held at one point a chair of histology at the Faculty of Medicine of Paris. The article in question was published in the *Journal de l'Anatomie et de la Physiologie Normales et Pathologiques de l'Homme et des Animaux* edited by Robin. On Richet and hypnosis, see Estingoy and Ardiet (2005) and Gauld (1992, pp. 298–302).

[8] This is a reference to German physiologist Rudolf Heidenhain (1834–1897). Richet refers to Jean-Martin Charcot's (1825–1893) famous and highly influential hypnosis work (e.g., Charcot, 1882), which founded a theoretical approach to hypnosis that caused many controversies (see Nicolas, 2004). Physician Albert Ruault (1850-1928) later became known as a skeptic of the phenomena of mental suggestion (Ruault, 1886).

[9] For a bibliography of Richet's early physiological work, see Richet (1894; see also Wolf, 1993).

[10] See Richet (1883). Théodule Ribot (1839–1916) was a French philosopher who had much influence on the rise of empirical psychology in Nineteenth Century France. He edited the *Revue Philosophique de la France et de l'Étranger*, an important French forum for articles about philosophy, psychology, and various social sciences, and one which was unusually open during the Nineteenth Century to discussions of psychic phenomena (Alvarado & Evrard, 2013; Nicolas & Murray, 1999).

[11] Once a Councilor to the Czar, Russian Alexander Aksakof (1832–1903), whose name has various spellings in the literature, did much work in psychical research. He is not generally considered to be a psychologist. Perhaps Richet referred to him as a psychologist due to his interest in phenomena such as mediumship.

[12] Palladino not only influenced Richet's beliefs, but those of many other individuals as well, not to mention the development of research techniques and theoretical concepts (Alvarado, 1993). Early overviews of her

mediumship were presented by Carrington (1909) and by de Rochas (1896, pp. 1–315). Aksakof was one of the organizers of the famous 1892 seances with this medium (Aksakof et al., 1893, Richet 1893a), which brought her mediumship to international attention. The names Richet mentioned were Italian scientists who attended some or most of the séances: criminologist and psychiatrist Cesare Lombroso (1836–1909), astronomer Giovanni Schiaparelli (1835–1910), physicist Giuseppe Gerosa (1857–1910), and physicist Giorgio Finzi (1868–1958). In addition to Aksakof, others attended as well but were not mentioned by Richet: Italian philosopher Angelo Brofferio (1846–1894), German philosopher Carl du Prel (1839–1899), and Italian physicist Giovanni Battista Ermacora (1858–1898).

[13] On these seances, see Lodge (1894) and Richet (1895). It may be that after the Palladino seances Richet became more involved with psychic phenomena, but readers should be aware that before these sittings he had shown considerable interest in psychic phenomena (Richet, 1884b, 1888, 1889).

[14] This was reported by Richet (1884b, pp. 651–653, see also Richet, n.d., pp. 87–89). A clearer description of this test was presented by Richet elsewhere:

> G., the medium, placed his hands on the table, every tilt setting in motion an electric bell. C. and D. also had their hands on the table but did not influence it. At three or four yards' distance on another table, and behind; sheet of cardboard, the alphabet was placed so that G., who had his back turned to it, could not see it. A. and B. sit at this table runs over the alphabet with a pencil, B. writes down the letter at which the table tilts, he being made aware of this by the sound of the bell. The letters indicated by this method give intelligible sentences; therefore, the tilts being due to unconscious

muscular pressure by G., these pressures, indicating the letter required, must be due to lucidity. Everything happens as if G., wanting to send a message, could see the alphabet to which his back is turned and which is hidden by the cardboard sheet. The movement of the pencil over the letters is both silent and irregular, and during these experiments we intentionally talk, sing, recite verses, and in fact make such a noise that B., who writes down the letters, can hardly hear the stroke of the bell. (Richet, 1923, pp. 168–169)

[15] Richet here refers to the SPR, founded in London in 1882 (Gauld, 1968).The persons mentioned are among the most important early members of the Society: intellectual Edmund Gurney (1847–1888), classical scholar Frederic W. H. Myers (1843–1901), moral philosopher Henry Sidgwick (1838–1900), and physicist Oliver J. Lodge (1851–1940). The first major work of the SPR was *Phantasms of the Living* (Gurney, Myers, & Podmore, 1886), an examination of possible cases of telepathy, presenting hundreds of cases of veridical manifestations.

[16] Ochorowicz (1850–1917) was a Polish psychologist and philosopher, as well as a psychical researcher. On his seances with Richet, see Lodge (1894) and Richet (1895).

[17] This is a reference to Italian physiologist Filippo Bottazzi (1867–1941), Italian pathologist Pio Foà (1848–1923), Italian physiologist Amedeo Herlitzka (1872–1949), English barrister Everard Feilding (1867–1936), the above-mentioned Frederic W. H. Myers, German physician Albert Schrenck-Notzing (1862–1929), French military engineer Albert Rochas (1837–1914), French astronomer Camille Flammarion (1842–1925), French physiologist Jacques-Arsène d'Arnsoval (1851–1940), French physicists Pierre Curie (1859–1906) and Marie Curie (1867–1934), and French psychologist Jules Courtier (1860–1938).

[18] In a paper published by the SPR, Richet said that after his initial Milan seances he was convinced of the reality of the phenomena but that about a fortnight after the events he had doubts (Richet, 1899, p.156).

[19] Richet (1901) expressed his admiration for Myers in an obituary. He believed Myers' work "perhaps will eclipse all other human knowledge" (p. 178).

[20] This sentence, and the next two paragraphs were in a footnote which call number appeared at the end of the previous paragraph in this paper (ending with footnote 19). Here Richet referred to his materialization séances with Marthe Béraud (Richet, 1905a), which brought much skepticism and many controversies at the time, too extensive to review here (for summaries and references, see Brower, 2010, pp. 84–92; Evrard, 2016, pp. 172–199, and Le Maléfan, 2002). The séances took place in Algiers at the villa of General Elie Noël (1835–1915) and his wife Carmencita (1846–1907). The A. referred to in the account is the coachman Areski, who was seen by Gabriel Delanne (1857-1926) attempting fraud (Delanne, 1905, p. 258).

Richet's account in *Souvenirs* presented here in translation does not include many other details and accusations, including his contemporary counter-critiques, which I have avoided discussing here (see Evrard, 2016, pp. 172–199). Regardless of the interpretation of the incident, these accusations, and the séances in general, caused much skepticism and affected Richet's reputation, something that is not evident in Richet's short comment. He defended the validity of his observations in several publications (e.g., Richet, 1922, pp. 599, 642–650, 1925, p. 861).

[21] The address, entitled "La Métapsychique," was presented in 1905, not in 1885, and published in the SPR *Proceedings* (Richet, 1905b). In a footnote in the address (p. 13) Richet acknowledged the prior use of the term by Polish philosopher Wincenty Lutosławski (1863–1954).

22 The term was used mainly in France, and to some extent in a few other (mainly European) countries, but it was not widely used in English.

23 As is well-known, Crookes (1832–1919) was an English chemist and physicist interested in the phenomena of Spiritualism, particularly the physical ones. Richet (1905b, p. 7) admired Crookes' scientific courage in discussing controversial topics, and believed that Crookes' studies were of fundamental importance for physical mediumship (Richet, 1922, p. 35).

24 This refers to English medium William Eglinton (1857–1933), and American mediums Henry Slade (1835–1905) and Leonora E. Piper (1857–1950).

25 Ossowiecki was a famous Polish psychic. Richet (n.d., pp. 148–162) gave a summary of his experiences with this psychic.

26 Actually, some mental phenomena have been discussed with Palladino (Venzano 1906). Similarly there were rare physical phenomena with Ossowiecki (Barrington, Stevenson, & Weaver, 2005, p. 23).

27 As seen in the previous chapter Richet (e.g., 1922, 1924) wrote repeatedly about his views about survival. I am grateful to Renaud Evrard for pointing out to me that Carroy (2015) has argued that Richet was more positive about spiritist interpretations in his literary fiction works dealing with psychic phenomena (on the latter see also Carroy, 2004).

28 Meyer (1855–1931) was a French industrialist and spiritist who funded the Institut Métapsychique International (1919). The other men, all involved with psychical research in France, were physician Gustave Geley (1868–1924), physician Eugène Osty (1874–1938), chemical engineer René Warcollier (1881–1962), and physician Jean-Charles Roux (1872–1942).

29 This paragraph and the next sentence are separated from the text and may have been meant as a short conclusion to the book, and not as a commentary about metapsychics.

30 At the end of his *Traité*, Richet stated that regardless of difficulties in understanding psychic phenomena there "is no reason for not increasing our efforts and labors. … The task is so beautiful that, even if we fail, the honor of having undertaken it gives some value to life" (Richet, 1922, p. 793).

31 Renaud Evrard suggested to me that it would be interesting to compare the chapter presented here with Richet's previously written but unpublished *Mémoires sur Moi et sur les Autres*, held at the Fonds Richet of the Académie National de Médicine (Retrieved from http://www.calames.abes.fr/pub/anm.aspx#details?id=FileId-363), which I have not seen. In fact Evrard, who has done much research about Richet (Evrard, 2016, Chapter 5), suggested to me the possibility that Richet used the *Mémoires* to write *Souvenirs*.

Chapter 4

1 Some examples are the publications of Alvarado (2009, 2014, 2017), Coon (1992), Evrard, Pratte, & Cardeña (2018), Le Maléfan (1995), and Sommer (2012, 2013).

2 The congresses have been discussed by many writers (e.g., Piéron, 1954; Sava, 2010). But only two have focused on psychical research (Alvarado, 2017; Taves, 2014)

3 There were many discussions in some of the congresses (e.g., Statistique des Hallucinations, 1890; Sidgwick, 1892) of what later became known as the Census of Hallucinations (Sidgwick et al., 1894).

4 As mentioned in a previous chapter, Richet presented the word in his 1905 Presidential Address to the Society for Psychical Research (Richet, 1905b). In a footnote of the published paper (p. 13) he acknowledged that the term had been used before.

5   There were comprehensive treatises of psychical research in later years, as seen in Richet's (1922) own work, and in the works of Moser (1935) and Sudre (1926). But Richet's prediction that psychic phenomena "will have conquered for itself a right to the light of day" in a few years was not fulfilled.

6   In this year, Richet published a paper that is important for the history of hypnosis in France (Richet, 1875). On this paper see Estingoy and Ardiet (2005).

7   Carroy and Schmidgen (2006, p. 200) suggest that Wundt was defensive regarding psychological research using hypnosis because he may have felt that his own approach to psychology could be marginalized. On Wundt's negative attitude towards hypnotic experimentation and psychic phenomena see his short book (Wundt, 1892/2000) and other writings (e.g., Marshall & Went, 1980).

Chapter 5

1   There are also translations into other languages such as German (Richet, 1923a), and Spanish (Richet, 1923c).

2   For an overview of the previous literature on these ideas see Alvarado (2006).

3   This refers to Karl Ludwig von Reichenbach's (1788–1869) discussions of an universal force he called Od, and Albert de Rochas' (1837–1914) studies of the exteriorization of tactile sensations beyond the confines of the human body (de Rochas, 1899; Reichenbach, 1849/1851). Mention of old magnetizers refers to early mesmerists and their ideas of animal magnetism, among them Joseph-Philippe-François Deleuze (1753–1835) (Deleuze, 1813).

4   A critic in the leading French spiritist journal *Revue Spirite* commented on Richet's materialistic assumptions,

and apparent contradictions in some statements in which he was trying to be less negative about survival (Bénézech, 1922). To counter Richet's belief in the banality of spirit communications, he argued for a consideration of the great difficulties of spirits to communicate via mediums. A more cohesive critique was presented by physician Gustave Geley (1865–1924), who disagreed with Richet's materialistic tenets arguing that consciousness, and functions such as memory, did not depend on the nervous system (Geley, 1922). Writing in the spiritualist journal *Light* several writers were puzzled by Richet's doubts about survival of death (e.g., Curnow, 1923; Stephens, 1923).

5   Other publications that had reviews of the book included *Bibliothèque Universelle et Revue Suisse* (F., 1922), *Journal de Débats Politiques et Littéraires* (de Varigny, 1922), *Revue des Deux Mondes* (Nordmann, 1922), *Polybiblion: Revue Bibliographique Universelle* (Ferrand, 1922), *Revue Bibliographique* (Anonymous, 1922b), *Revue de la Semaine Illustrée* (Guitet-Vauquelin, 1922), and the *Rivista de Psicologia* (Ferrari, 1922).

6   For discussions of examples of rejection of psychic phenomena for different reasons see Alvarado (2017), Coon (1992), Marmin (2001), and Sommer (2013). All of this is consistent with "boundary work", or strategies of rejection of ideas, or particular work, that a specific group feels is a threat to their own status. It is conceptual and methodological rejection "for the purpose of drawing a rhetorical boundary between science and some less authoritative residual non-science" (Gieryn, 1999, pp. 4–5).

7   Related to this is Richet's (1922b, p. ii) claim that he prepared the book following the style of treatises from other disciplines.

8   Althought Richet distanced himself from belief in discarnate agency in many publications (e.g., Richet,

1924), his similar stance about this in the *Traité* may be seen as a device to legitimize the scientific approach of metapsychics in face of fields such as medicine, physics, and psychology that had superseded such conceptions. He stated that he wanted to "remove from the facts called occult … the supernatural and mystical appearance attributed by people who do not deny them" (Richet, 1922b, p. ii).

9   Heuzé's well-known articles were compiled into books that helped to popularize their message even more (Heuzé, 1921b, 1922c).

10 Some examples were Flammarion (1920–1922), Geley (1924/1927), and Osty (1922/1923).

Chapter 6

1   On psychopathology see the studies of Alvarado and Zingrone (2012) and Le Maléfan (1999).

2   See the discussions of these issues by Alvarado (2011, 2016), Maraldi and Alvarado (2018), and Sudre (1946).

3   On the idea of human supernormal agency to explain mental and physical mediumship see Alvarado (2014) and Alvarado, Nahm, and Sommer (2012).

4   Hélène Smith (pseudonym of Catherine Elise Müller) was a medium [who was] investigated by the above mentioned psychololologist Théodore Flournoy (1900). Flournoy gave psychological explanations for the medium's mediumistic romances of a previous life in France, in India, as well as of life on Mars. Both Smith and Flournoy are discussed by Shamdasani (1994; see also Alvarado, Maraldi, Machado, & Zangari, 2014; and Maraldi & Alvarado, 2018).

5   Spiritist critiques of Flournoy's study have been reviewed by Alvarado and Zingrone (2015).

6   Richet (1923) described Stella as "young lady who is not
     a professional medium and only took up spiritualism by
     chance" (p. 147, her phenomena are discussed on pages
     147–149).

7   Richet (1923) defined the term in a footnote: "I propose
     pantomnesia to indicate that no vestige of our intellectual
     past is entirely effaced. Probably we are all pantomnesic.
     In weighing metapsychic facts it should be taken for
     granted that we do not absolutely forget anything that
     has once impressed our senses" (p. 52).

8   Victorien Sardou (1831–1908) was a well-known
     French playwright. He wrote about his mediumistic
     communications and drawings of houses in Jupiter
     where both Mozart and Zoroaster lived (Sardou, 1858).
     His interests in spiritism has been discussed by Hart
     (1913, Chapter 12). According to Flammarion (1907),
     "my illustrious friend Victorien Sardou ... had written,
     as a medium, some curious pages on the inhabitants of
     the planet Jupiter, and had produced picturesque and
     surprising designs, having as their aim to represent
     men and things as they appeared in this giant of worlds
     ... One of his sketches showed us the house of Mozart,
     others the houses of Zoroaster and of Bernard Palissy
     [a French 16th century ceramist and glassworker], who
     were country neighbors in one of the landscapes of this
     immense planet ..." (p. 25). Following on the tradition
     of conventional explanations, Flammarion argued that
     these productions did not come from spirits, but were
     the result of the medium's resources: "A person is not
     magnetized, nor hypnotized, nor put to sleep in any way
     while in that state. But the brain is not ignorant of what
     is taking place: its cells perform their functions, and act
     (doubtless by a reflex movement) upon the motor nerves.
     At that time we all thought Jupiter was inhabited by a
     superior race of beings. The spiritistic communications
     were the reflex of the general ideas in the air" (p. 26)

9 As mentioned in the first chapter, Richet (1884, 1888, 1889) had discussed the topic in previous papers in which he reported several experiments.

10 On this topic see Alvarado (2010, 2016), Carroy (1993), and Crabtree (1993). Myers (1903) saw the phenomena in question as more than mere conventional explanations. In his view these phenomena presented gradations of actions of a subliminal self closely related to phenomena such as telepathy and mediumship and to the issue of survival of bodily death.

Index

⁓

Note: Page number entries with an "N' are directing the reader to Notes; e.g. "177n11" means page 177 and note 11.

A

Abregé d'histoire générale, 151, 146, 153, 168

Académie de Médicine, 2, 80

Académie des Sciences, xv, 2, 76, 80

Adrienne, 30

Aksakof, Alexander, 15-16, 86, 105, 146, 152, 169, 177n11, 177-178n12

Albert I, Prince of Monaco, 28

Alice, 10, 32, 40, 71

Animal magnetism, 32, 60, 176n6, 183n3

Annales des sciences psychiques, 6, 41, 121, 126-129, 134, 146-147, 150, 152, 156

Areski, 41, 180n20

L'aviation triomphante, 3, 151

autobiography, limitations of, 41-43

B

Barrett, William, 48, 54, 109, 140, 157

Beaujon Hospital, 31

Béraud, Marthe, 6, 17, 18, 25, 72, 82, 103, 106, 180n20

H

L

J

K

L

S

www.ingramcontent.com/pod-product-compliance
Lightning Source LLC
Chambersburg PA
CBHW020154090426
42734CB00008B/819